THE CENTER FOR CARTOON STUDIES PRESENTS

HOUDINI
THE HANDCUFF KING

Jason Lutes & Nick Bertozzi

with an introduction by Glen David Gold

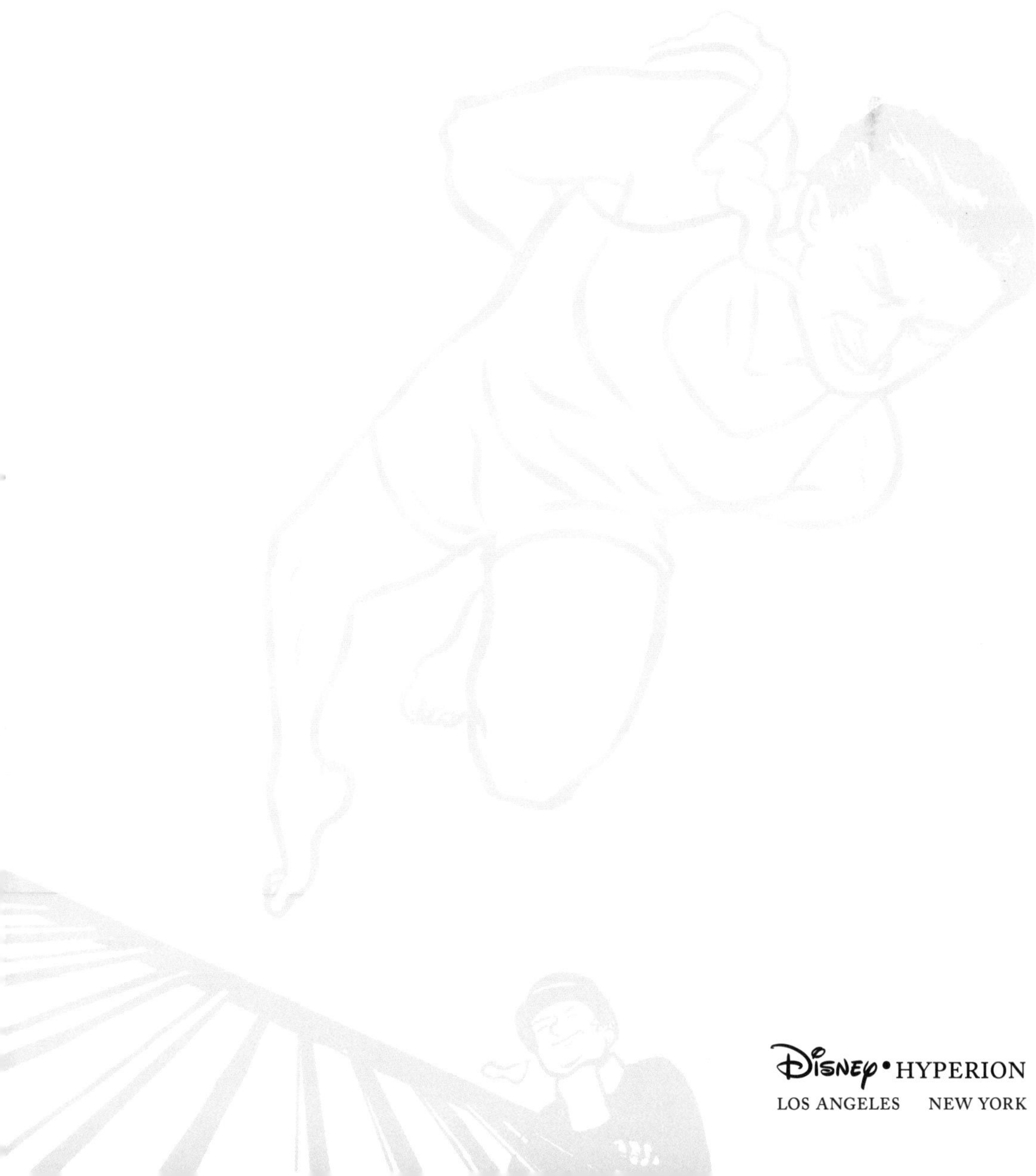

Disney • HYPERION
LOS ANGELES NEW YORK

First Hardcover Edition, April 2007
Second Hardcover Edition, September 2019
First Paperback Edition, July 2008
Second Paperback Edition, September 2019
10 9 8 7 6 5 4 3 2 1
FAC-029191-19179
Printed in Malaysia

Comic hand-lettered
Remaining text set in Adobe Caslon Pro/Fontspring

Library of Congress Control Number for Hardcover: 2007276145
Hardcover ISBN 978-1-368-02231-6
Paperback ISBN 978-1-368-04288-8
Reinforced binding
Visit www.DisneyBooks.com

The Center for Cartoon Studies
P.O. Box 125
White River Junction, Vermont 05001
Visit www.cartoonstudies.org

Introduction

by Glen David Gold

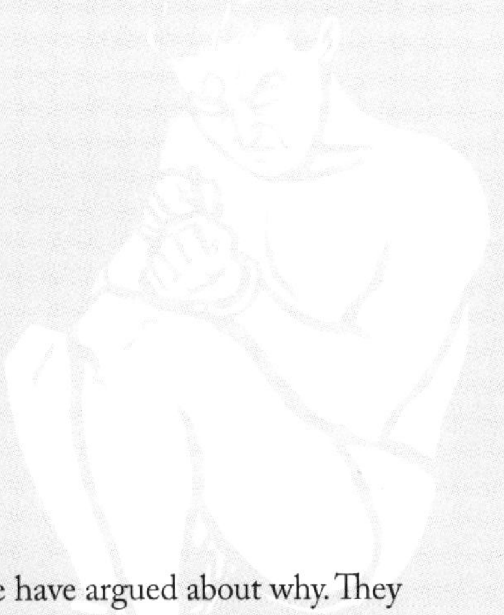

I cannot think of a more dangerous man to know than Mr. Harry Houdini, the man for whom the phrase "Kids, don't try this at home" might well have been invented. That his life and his secrets are described here in pictures and words is exciting indeed. It's as though someone has let a very powerful genie out of a very tight bottle. I would advise you to read this book carefully, several times, before deciding what exactly you think you have learned. You might discover that it's something to do with where the power of magic comes from.

Who was Houdini? A magician and an escape artist. Which might sound only moderately interesting but for the type of man he was. There are some people who, by the very force of their personal magnetism, make their field seem larger than it was before them. For instance, once upon a time, football and baseball were the sports most covered on the evening news. And then Michael Jordan started playing. After Michael Jordan, the world recognized how essentially thrilling basketball is. So it was with Houdini: once he had appeared onstage, the world paid attention to magic.

Not only could he escape from handcuffs, but he also escaped from ropes, straitjackets, police stations, coffins submerged underground, and infernal devices like the Chinese Water Torture Cell. He was, for a time, the most famous man in the world. For the past one hundred years, people have argued about why. They say that he appealed to the common person's sense of freedom, or of mystery, or of wonder, or that he was a perfect American success story. But the truth is, Houdini was the first man in history to be famous because what he did was cool.

Houdini, the son of a rabbi, was born Ehrich Weiss in Budapest, Hungary, in 1874. When he was still a toddler, his family moved to Wisconsin, in the heart of America. Discovering magic as a boy, he gave himself the stage name Harry Houdini to reflect his respect for Jean Eugène Robert-Houdin, a great French conjurer. Young Houdini's act was good, but not excellent, and at the time there were many, many magicians to compete with. He needed a way to make people talk about him.

At the beginning of the twentieth century, there was of course no Internet, no radio, no DVDs or CDs—there weren't really even movie theaters. Not yet. If you wanted to be entertained, it meant going out and seeing actual people performing onstage. If you wanted to laugh, you saw a comedian; if you wanted to cry, you saw a melodrama. But if you wanted to be amazed, your only real choice was to see a magician.

Houdini wanted to amaze people. He found that updating old magic techniques for escaping from ropes and chains onstage—and applying them to handcuffs—did the job. At the time, audiences weren't sure if magicians used sleight of hand, or if they were in league with demons and the supernatural. Not because audiences were stupid, but because in those days scientists kept coming up with amazing devices, like X-rays, and finding new species in the natural world, like gorillas, and discovering things not visible to the human eye, like germs and genes and radio waves. No one quite knew what was or wasn't possible anymore.

Houdini was one of the first magicians to announce that he performed all of his tricks simply because he was clever, physically fit, and agile. He challenged the audience to find stronger locks to hold him, and to their amazement, he escaped every time. No demons, no pacts with the devil. In other words, he celebrated being an ordinary man who was simply trying harder than anyone else. (This is why some people say his spirit was specifically American.)

If you were a rival of his, and made the mistake of declaring yourself a "Handcuff King," Houdini might show up at your performance and put you into a set of cuffs from which you couldn't escape, ending your career.

Realizing that just being a good magician wasn't enough, Houdini worked to become the greatest authority in the world on locks, handcuffs, and other restraints, and—of course—how to secretly pick them. He was highly competitive. If you were a rival of his, and made the mistake of declaring yourself a "Handcuff King," Houdini might show up at your performance and put you into a set of cuffs from which you couldn't escape, ending your career. The audience and the newspapers loved this. Houdini's name was reported everywhere. He traveled the world, thinking up new stunts to get his name in the papers, getting people into the theaters to see him perform.

Eventually, he moved beyond handcuffs,

inviting manufacturers to get free publicity by supplying things he could escape from: vises, mailbags, a giant lightbulb, and even a huge envelope, and a football sewn up around him. He also developed his own bizarre escapes. One of his signature performances, recorded in several newsreels, was to escape from a straitjacket while hanging upside down outside a building, many stories in the air, as thousands of people watched from below. The president at the time, Woodrow Wilson, congratulated him after such a show and said, "I wish I had your ability to get out of tight places."

This is another reason why people liked Houdini so much: he could do something no one else could, but everyone else *wanted* to. And escaping from impossible devices reminded people of how much they wanted to escape things—poverty, sorrow, illness—that also seemed hard to defeat. Houdini gave them hope.

Later in his life, this became even more important, because he was enraged by swindlers who only *pretended* to give people hope. In the 1920s, fortune-tellers known as mediums claimed they could talk to people's dead friends and relatives. They held séances, gatherings in small, dark rooms with heavy drapes, where musical instruments would float through the air, mysteriously playing themselves, while ghostly voices answered questions, apparently from beyond the grave. Houdini recognized what was going on: the mediums were using invisible wires, mirrors, and assistants hiding behind curtains—all old magicians' techniques. But they were claiming that they had supernatural powers, and they charged people money to talk to their dead relatives.

At first Houdini visited mediums as a client. He wished he could talk to his dead mother. When he realized the mediums were trying to fool him, he was incensed that anyone would try to victimize him.

For years, he gave lectures on spiritualists' tricks. He attended séances and broke them up when he sensed a fraud. He even coached scientists (who had been fooled themselves) in how to detect when a medium was faking. He had an epic battle with one woman, Margery, who was very good at evading him. She almost convinced *Scientific American*, a popular and respected magazine, to proclaim her a real medium. But finally Houdini caught her and showed how she had fooled everyone.

It's hard to know what it would have been like to know Houdini. He was loyal to his family and his friends, and demanded loyalty in return. With an almost unbelievable amount of energy, he was always ready for adventure. He was obsessive, working for hours and hours to figure out how a lock worked, or how to build a better onstage illusion. His passions meant he saw the world in black and white, and if you were on his wrong side, he could sometimes be a bully. He needed to prove he was the greatest showman in history, even if that meant bending the truth a bit. But he was also devoted: he adored his wife, Bess, as the story here shows.

Throughout his life, Houdini loved any sort of challenge. He wrote books, drove fast cars, piloted the first airplane in Australia, starred in movies, started the first magicians' organization, collected a vast and important library of obscure texts, and played to packed houses night after night. On his last tour, in 1926, something terrible happened: a backstage visitor asked if one of his feats of strength was the ability to take a punch to the stomach. No, not really, but it was a new challenge, so he said yes. The man punched him repeatedly before Houdini could brace himself.

Because he was stubborn and ignored everyone's advice, Houdini stayed away from the doctor for several days, even though he was in terrible agony. Finally, he was admitted to the hospital. His appendix had burst. After lingering, he died on October 31, 1926—Halloween.

For a man who could escape from anything, death was the ultimate challenge. Houdini had been fascinated by whether he could come back or not. His wife held séances every year on Halloween—séances that didn't use magic tricks—to see if his spirit could really be contacted. It never was.

But that wasn't the end of Houdini. People still talk about him. Whenever someone has a narrow escape from something, Houdini's name almost always comes up. And everyone still wonders how he did it. This book gives you some very interesting clues. But it also leaves some mysteries intact. How did he escape when Bess wasn't there? How did he manage to be buried alive? What were the secrets of the Milk-Can Escape? Of the Chinese Water Torture Cell? These might have been lost. Or someone, somewhere, might still have the answers, if you know where to look.

Houdini knew that knowledge is power. And no one just gives secrets away; that's why they stay secrets. By reading this book, you're getting a gift—you're learning just a little bit about how magic is done, and about how the greatest magician in the world managed one particular stunt. What you do with such knowledge is entirely up to you. But as I said, Houdini is a very dangerous man to know. He understood the value of mystery. On the one hand, he knew how mystery could be marketed as a way to get you into the theater. On the other, he knew that if you got to the theater and were disappointed, "mystery" would dissolve into "hype." The question "How does he do that?"—asked about Houdini, or Michael Jordan, or any performer in any field that you love—keeps mystery alive, and mystery is the fundamental source of wonder.

Enjoy!

—G.D.G.

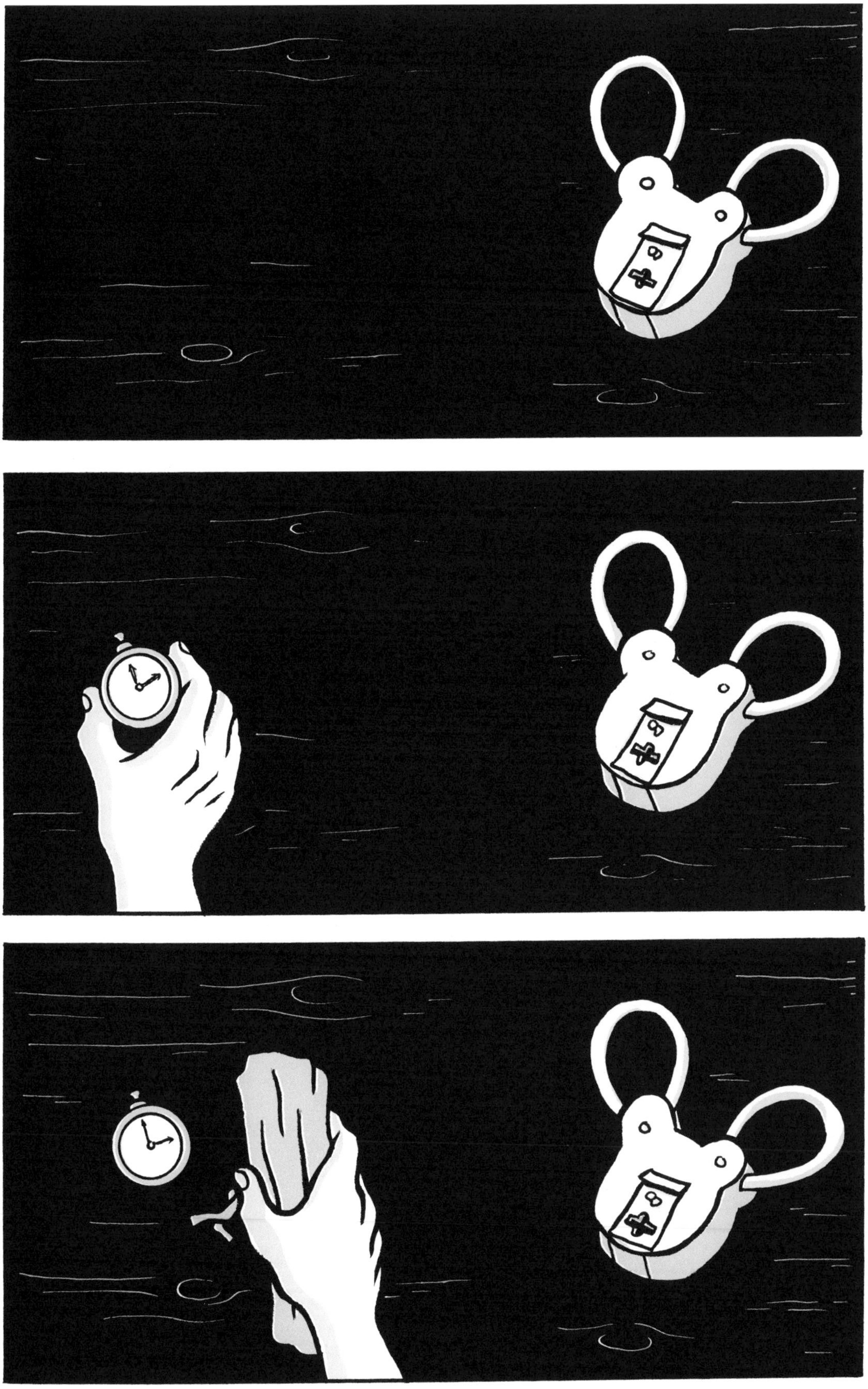

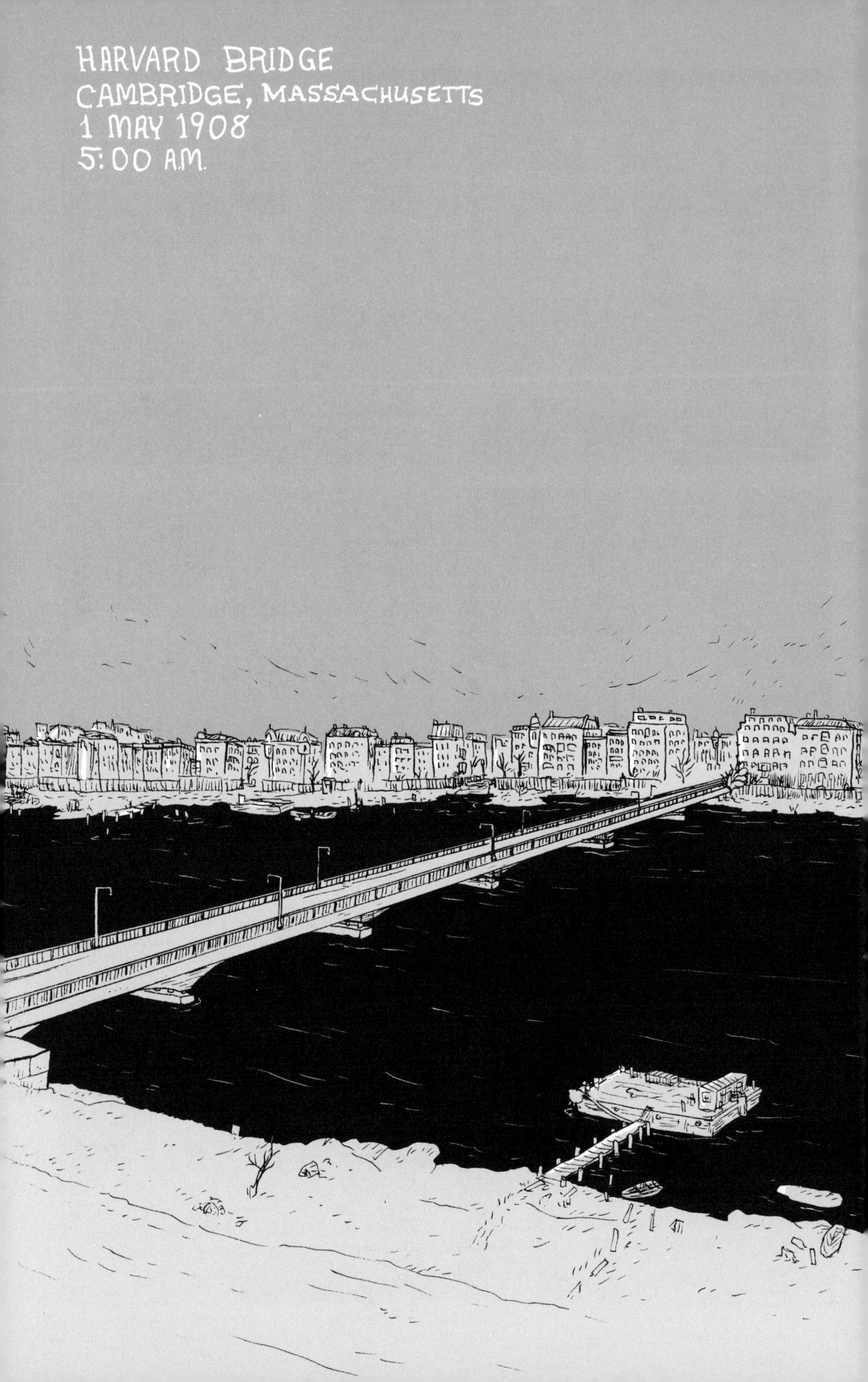
HARVARD BRIDGE
CAMBRIDGE, MASSACHUSETTS
1 MAY 1908
5:00 A.M.

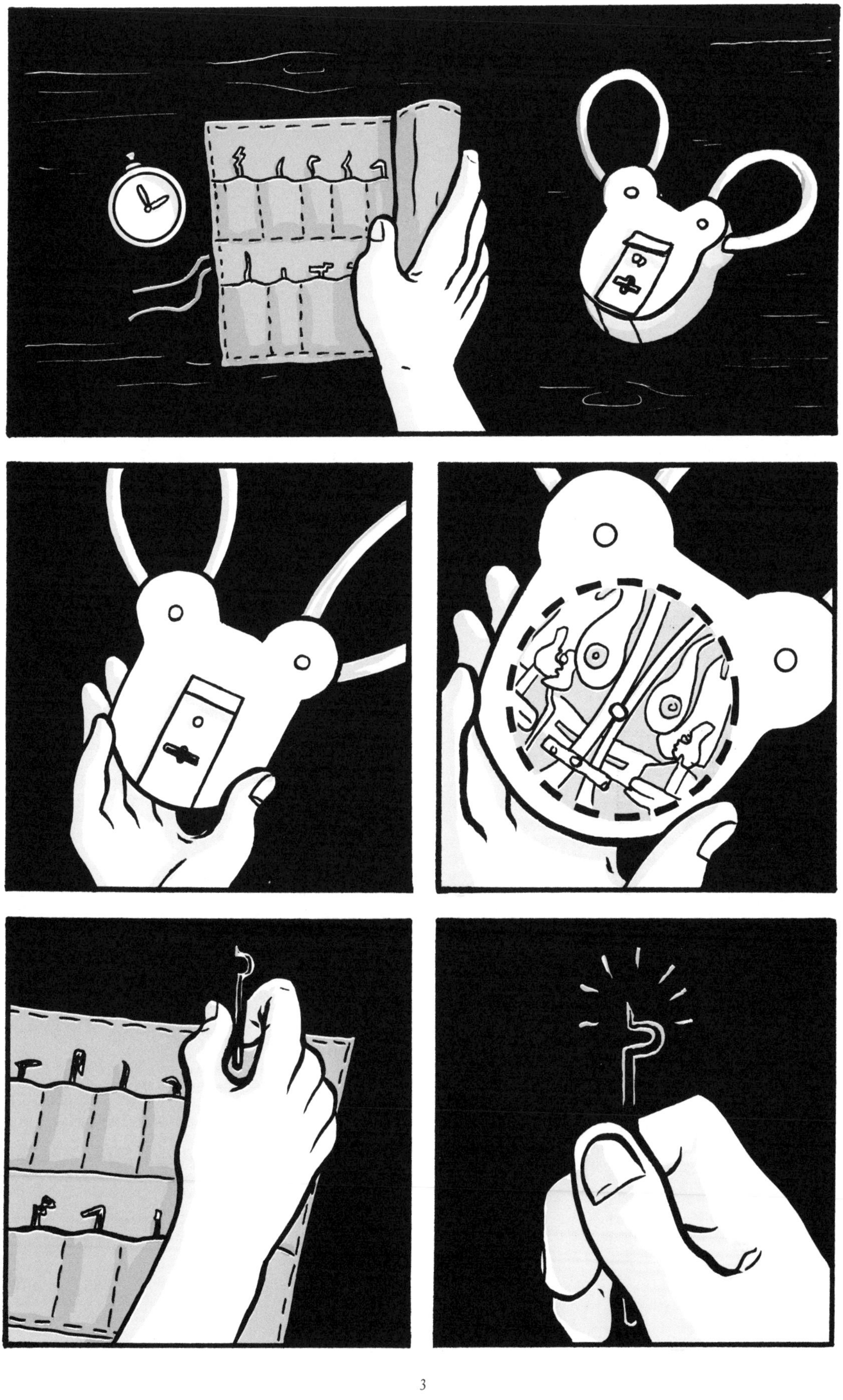

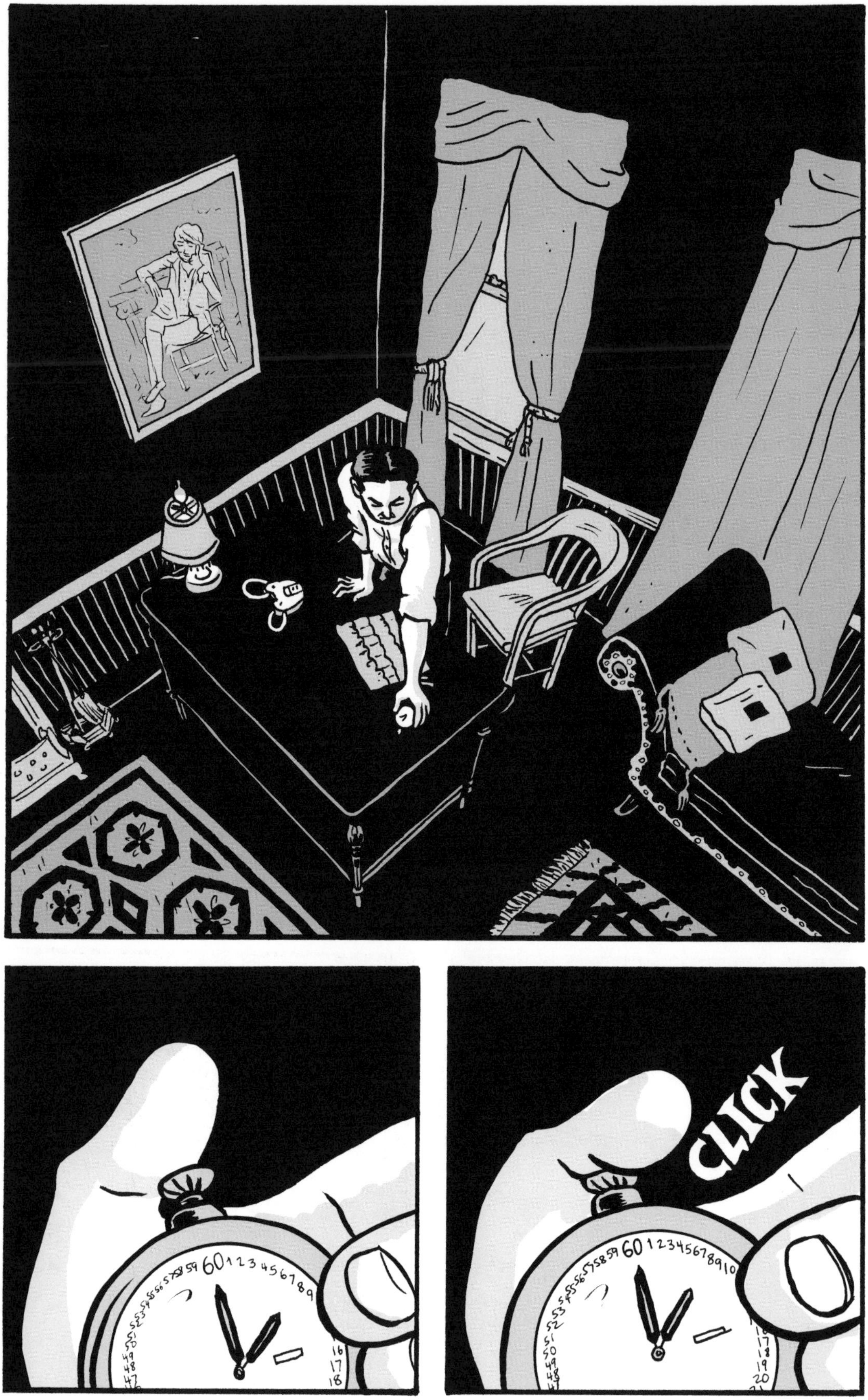
CLICK

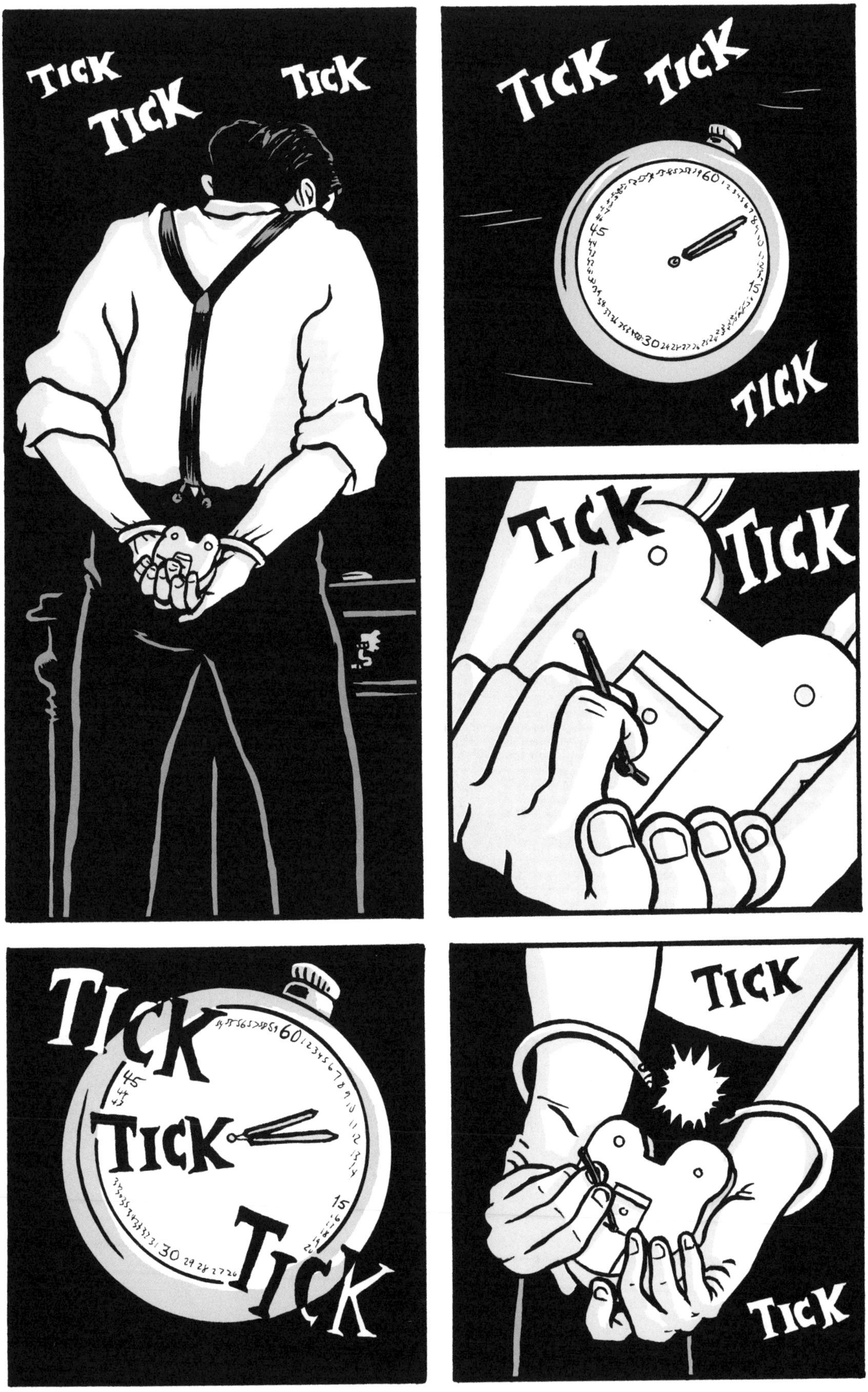
TICK
TICK
TICK
TICK
TICK
TICK
TICK
TICK
TICK
TICK
TICK
TICK
TICK

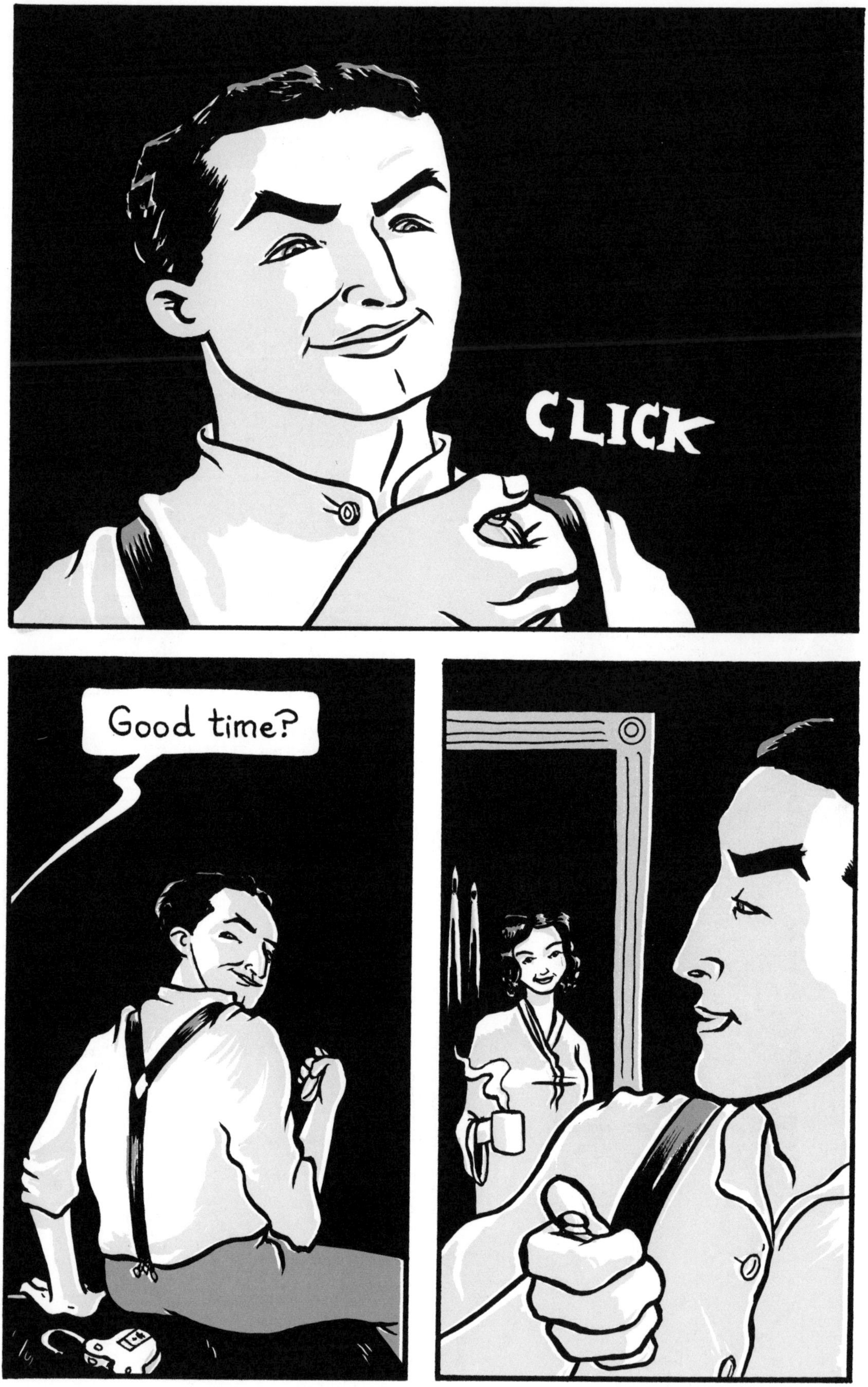
CLICK
Good time?

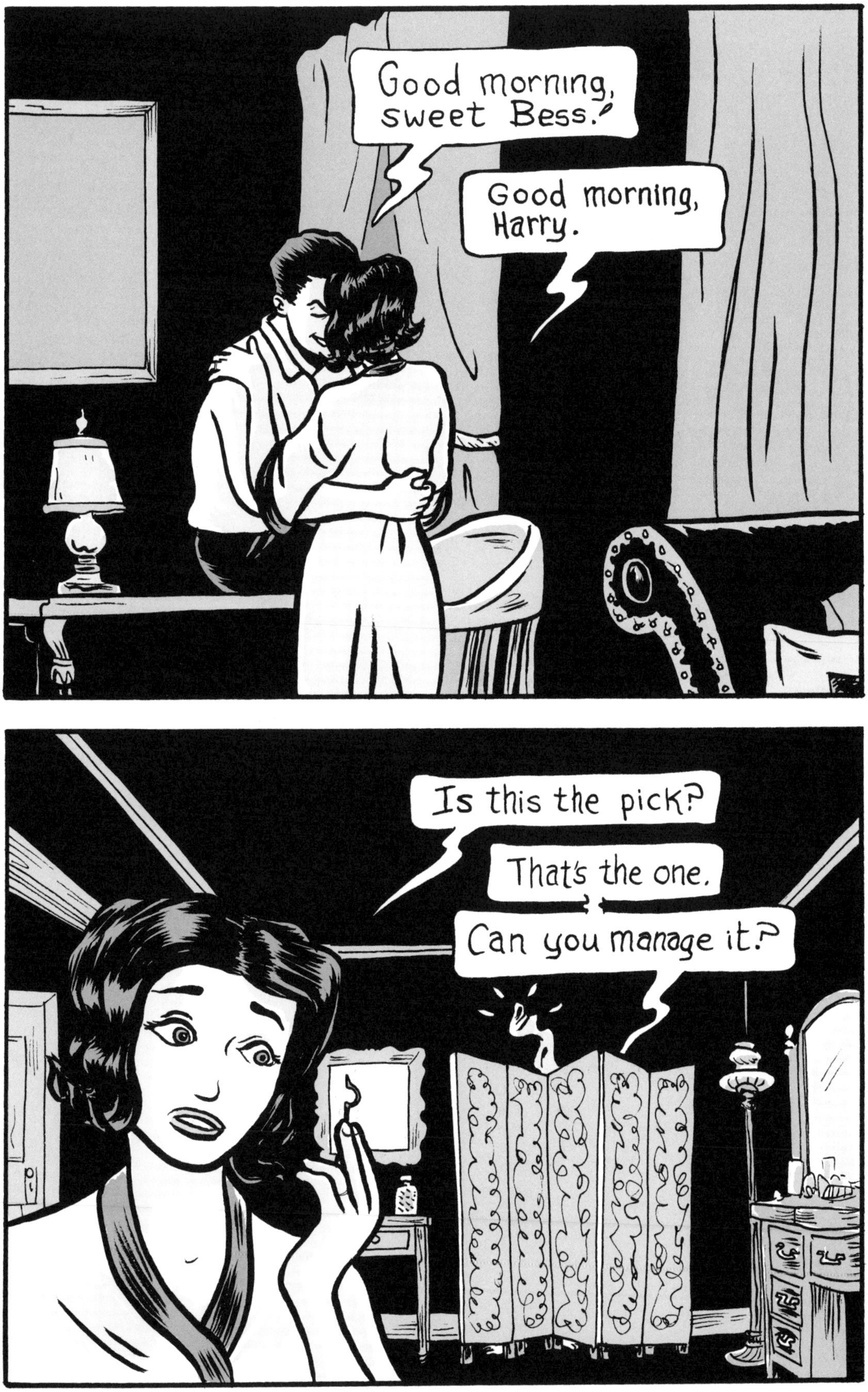
Good morning, sweet Bess.
Good morning, Harry.
Is this the pick?
That's the one.
Can you manage it?

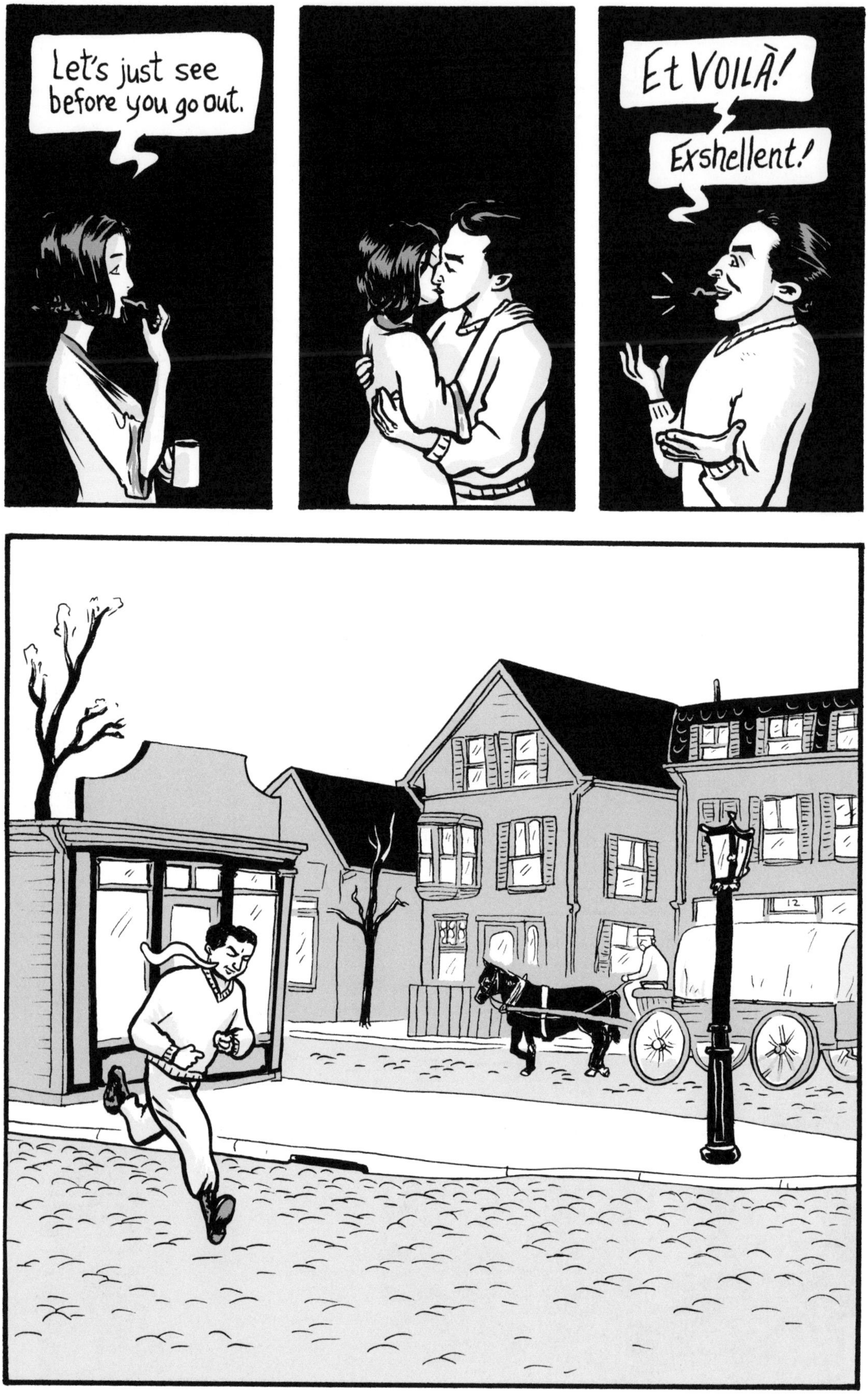
Let's just see before you go out.
Et VOILÀ!
Exshellent!

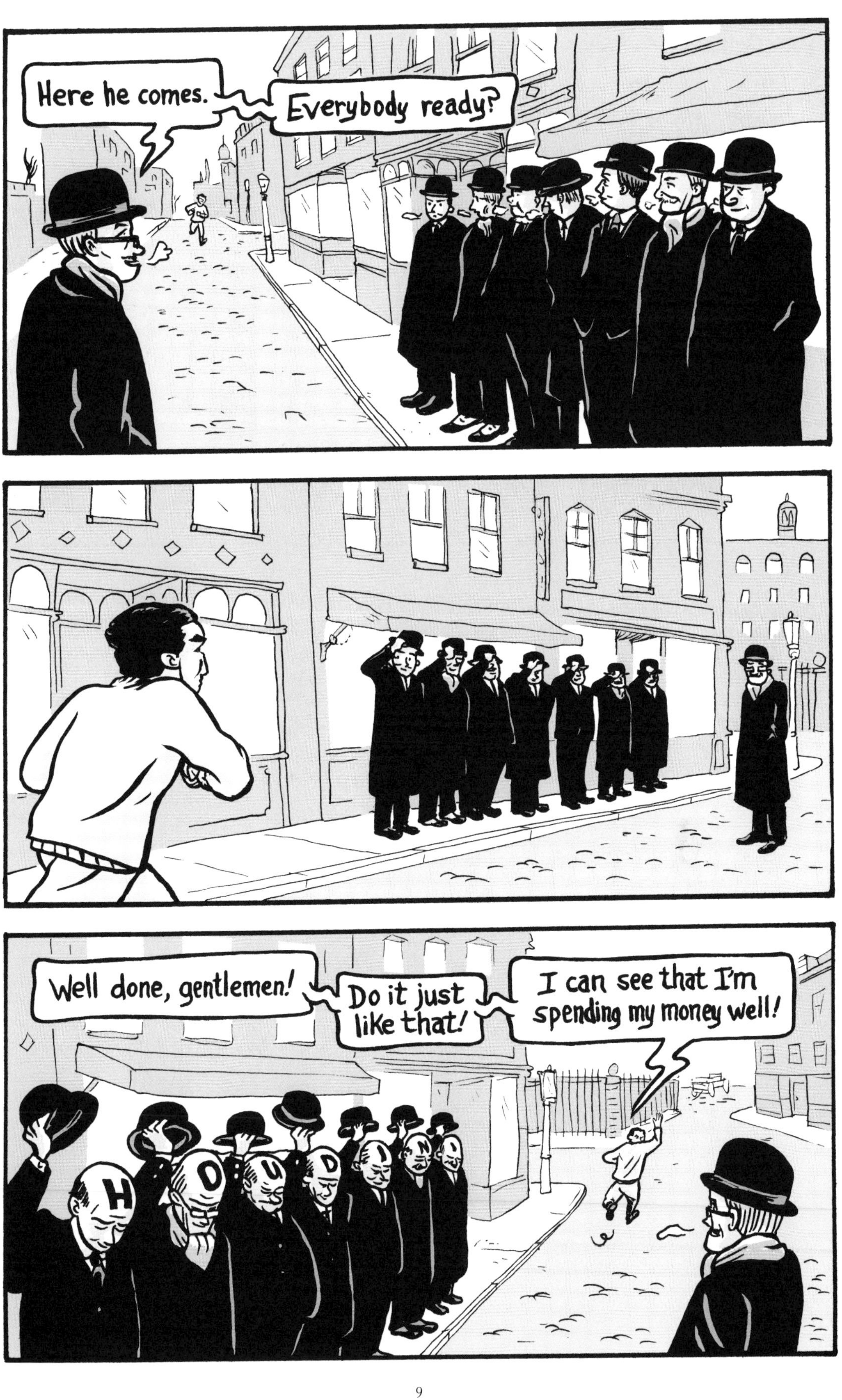
Here he comes.
Everybody ready?
Well done, gentlemen!
Do it just like that!
I can see that I'm spending my money well!
H O U D I N I

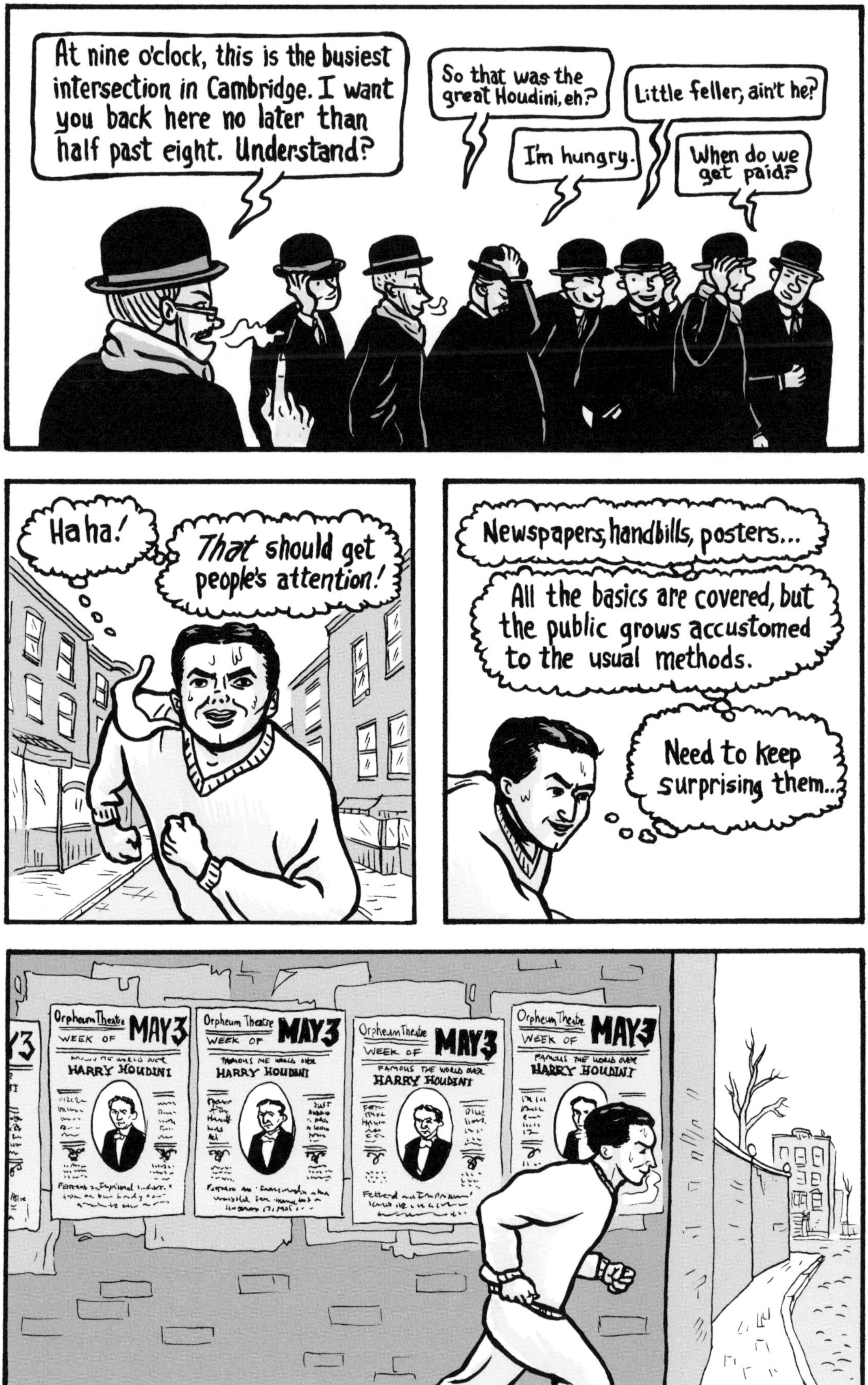
At nine o'clock, this is the busiest intersection in Cambridge. I want you back here no later than half past eight. Understand?
So that was the great Houdini, eh?
I'm hungry.
Little feller, ain't he?
When do we get paid?
Haha!
That should get people's attention!
Newspapers, handbills, posters...
All the basics are covered, but the public grows accustomed to the usual methods.
Need to keep surprising them...
Orpheum Theatre
WEEK OF
MAY 3
HARRY HOUDINI

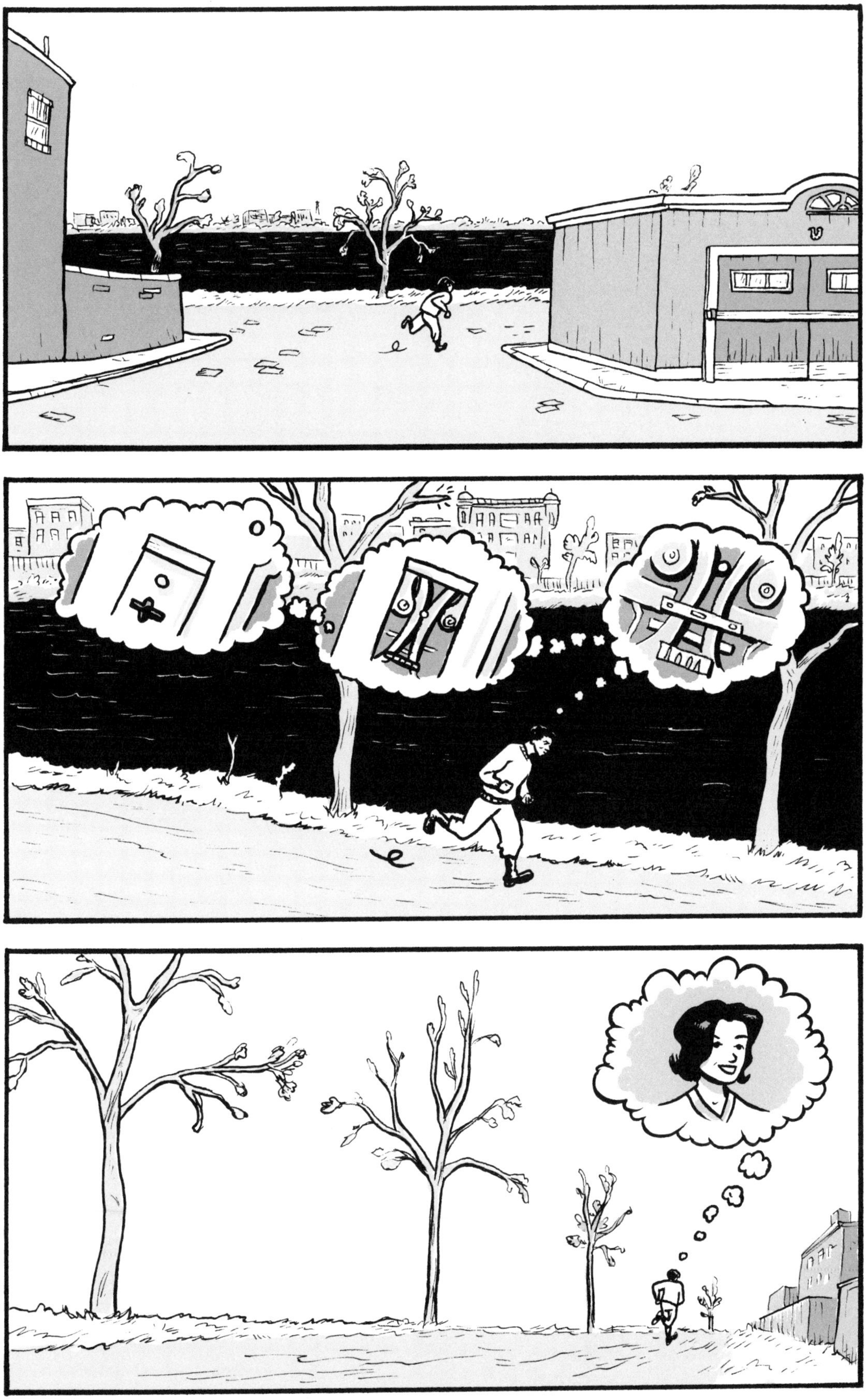

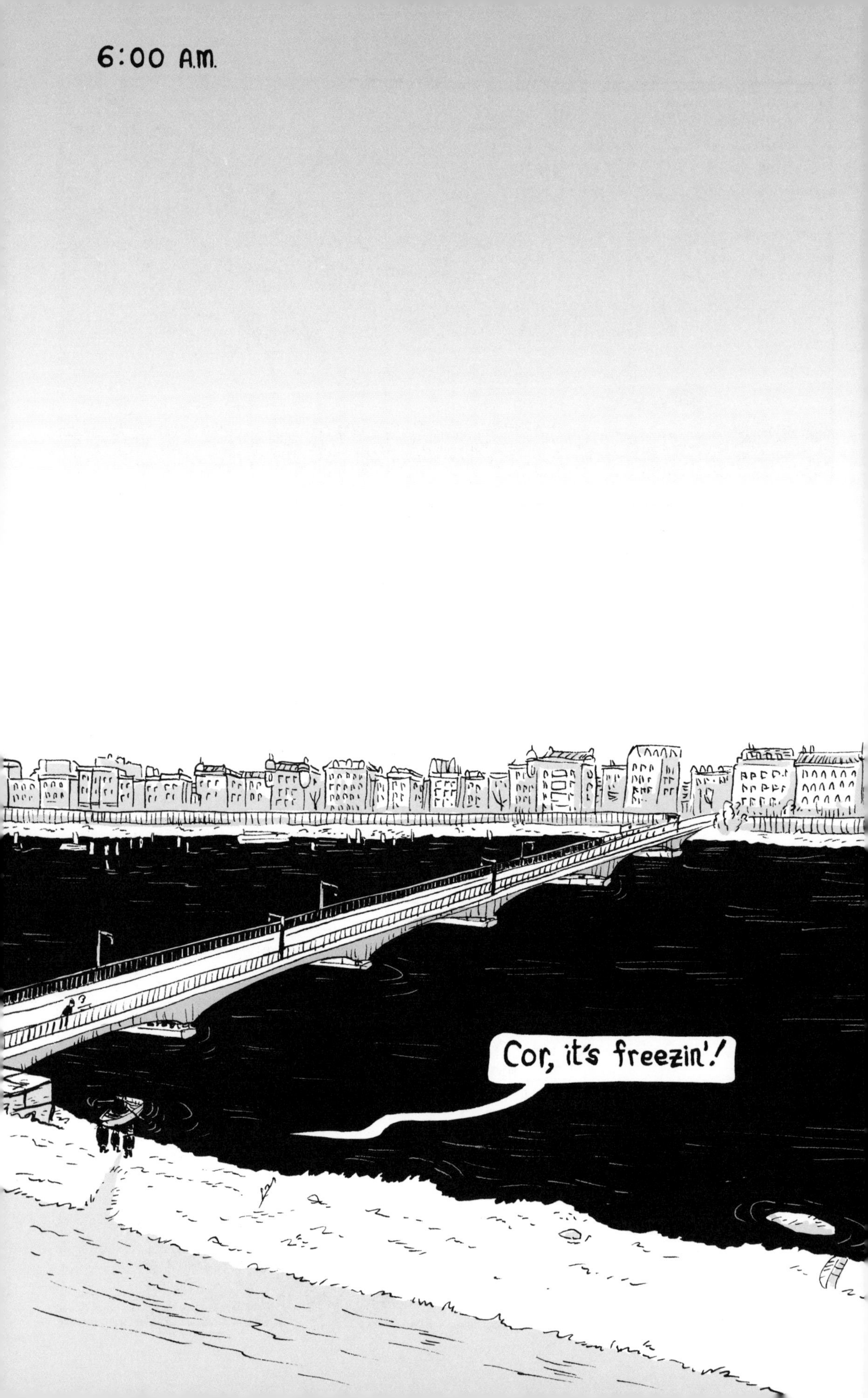
6:00 A.M.
Cor, it's freezin'!

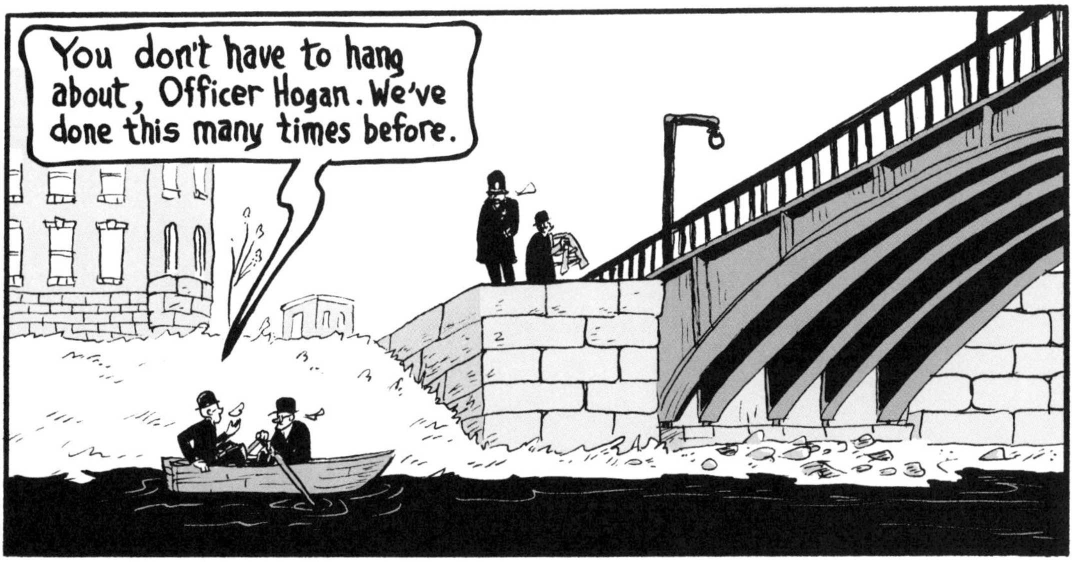
You don't have to hang about, Officer Hogan. We've done this many times before.
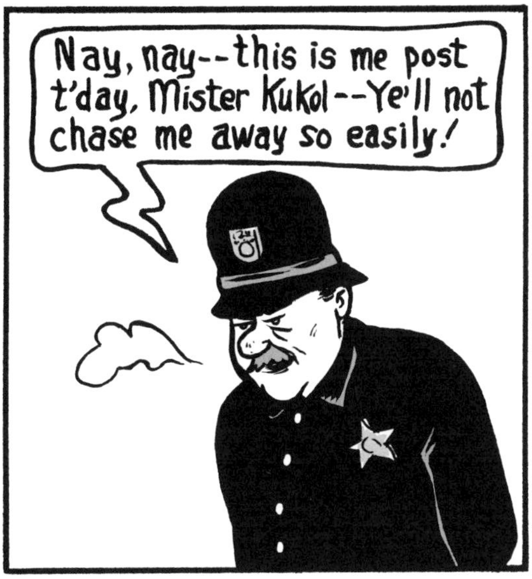
Nay, nay--this is me post t'day, Mister Kukol--Ye'll not chase me away so easily!
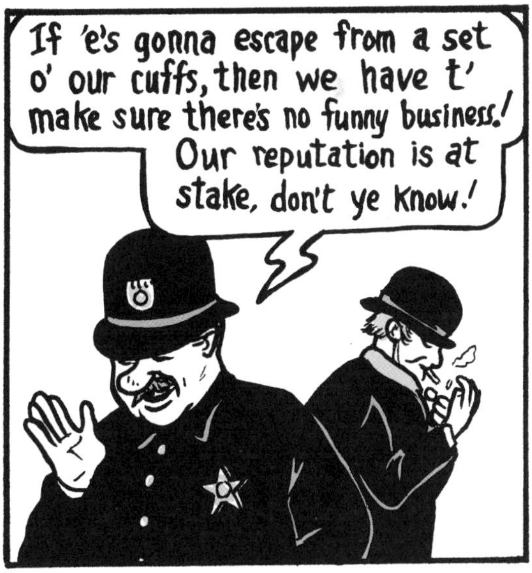
If 'e's gonna escape from a set o' our cuffs, then we have t' make sure there's no funny business!
Our reputation is at stake, don't ye know!
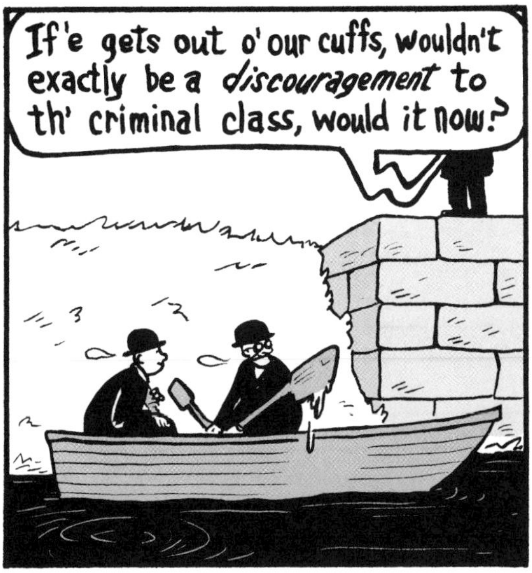
If 'e gets out o' our cuffs, wouldn't exactly be a *discouragement* to th' criminal class, would it now?
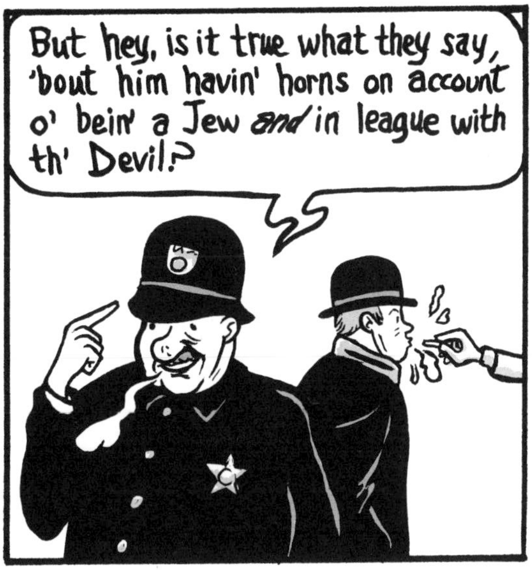
But hey, is it true what they say, 'bout him havin' horns on account o' bein' a Jew *and* in league with th' Devil?

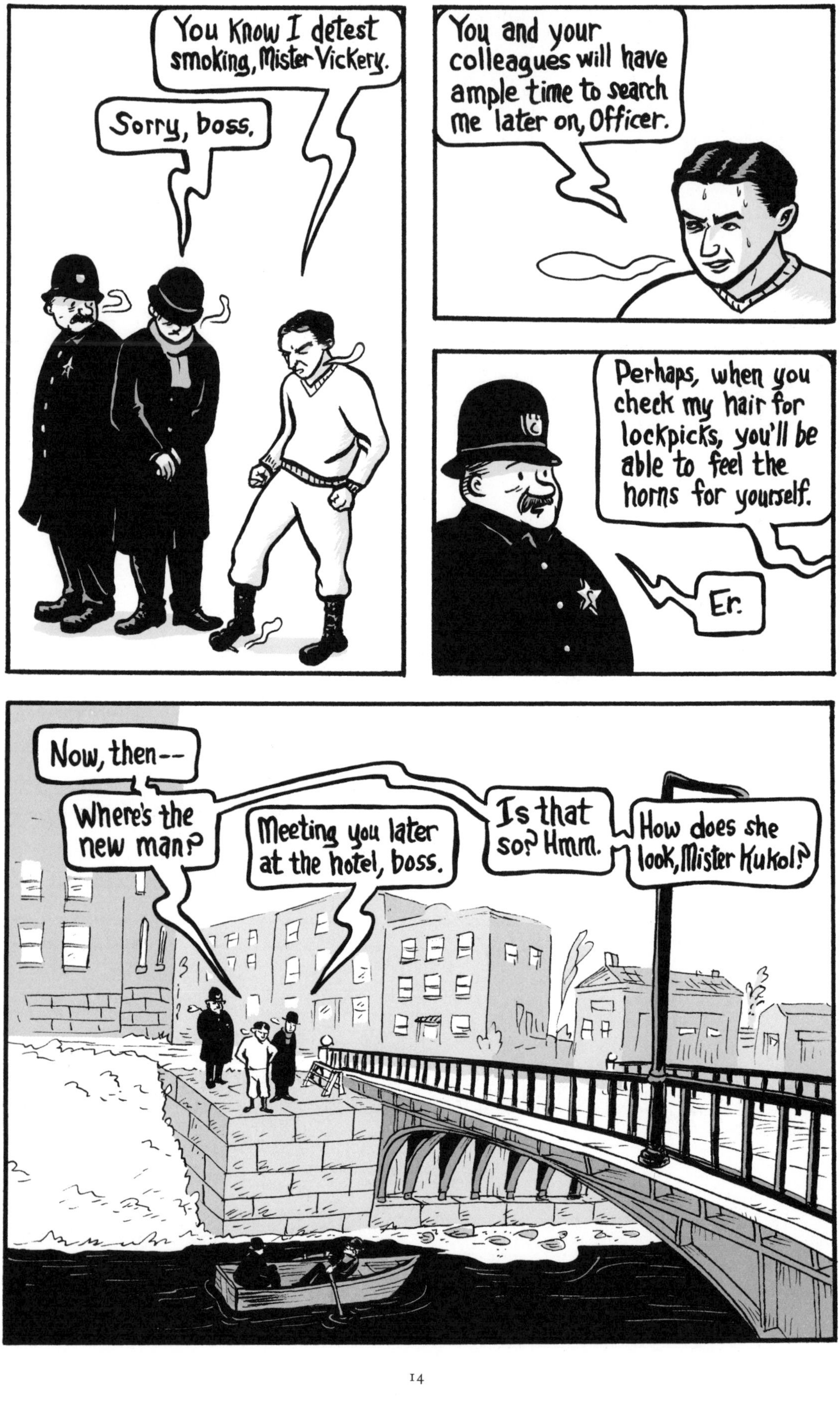
You Know I detest smoking, Mister Vickery.
Sorry, boss.
You and your colleagues will have ample time to search me later on, Officer.
Perhaps, when you check my hair for lockpicks, you'll be able to feel the horns for yourself.
Er.
Now, then--
Where's the new man?
Meeting you later at the hotel, boss.
Is that so? Hmm.
How does she look, Mister Kukol?

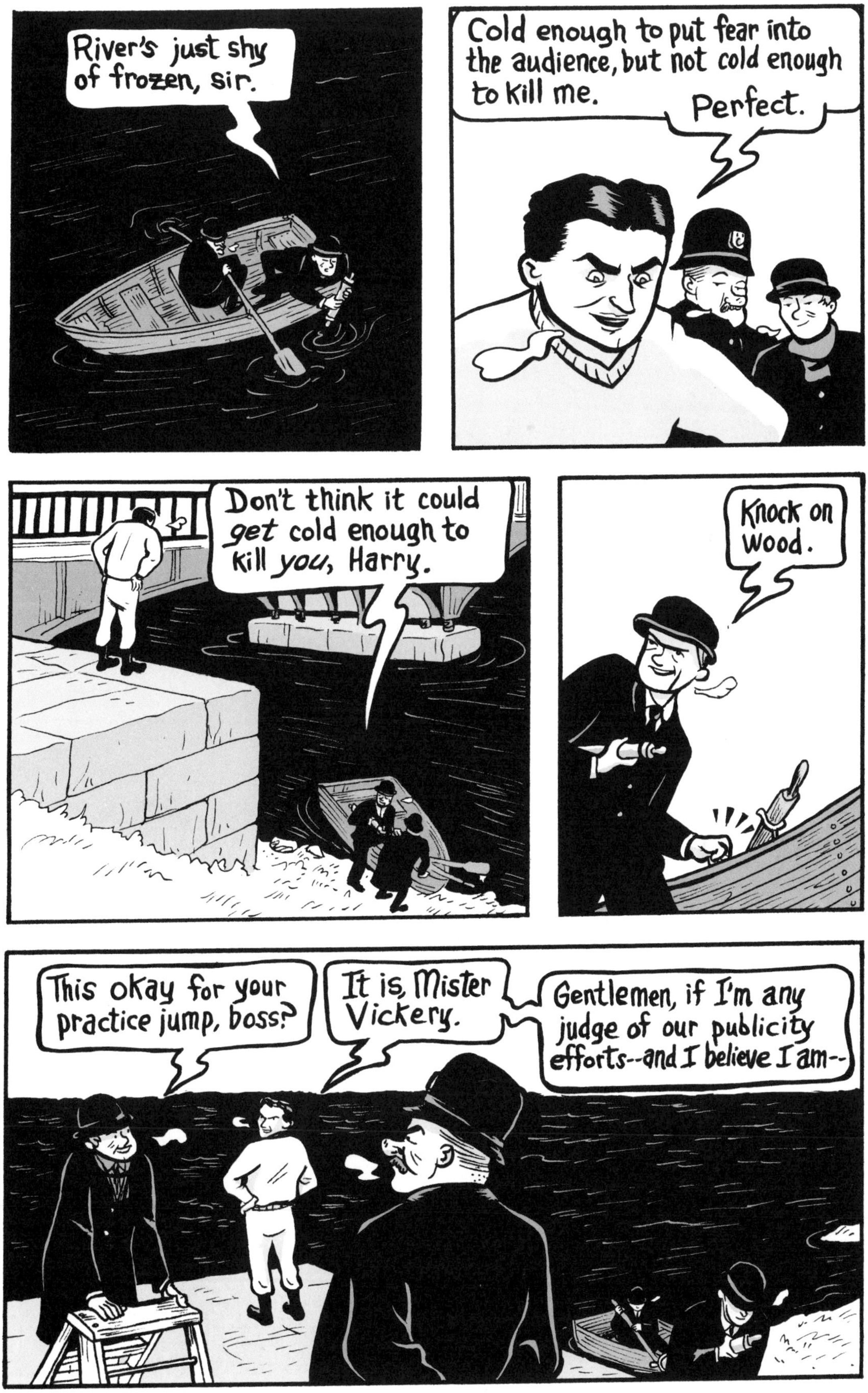
River's just shy of frozen, sir.
Cold enough to put fear into the audience, but not cold enough to kill me.
Perfect.
Don't think it could *get* cold enough to kill *you*, Harry.
Knock on wood.
This okay for your practice jump, boss?
It is, Mister Vickery.
Gentlemen, if I'm any judge of our publicity efforts--and I believe I am--

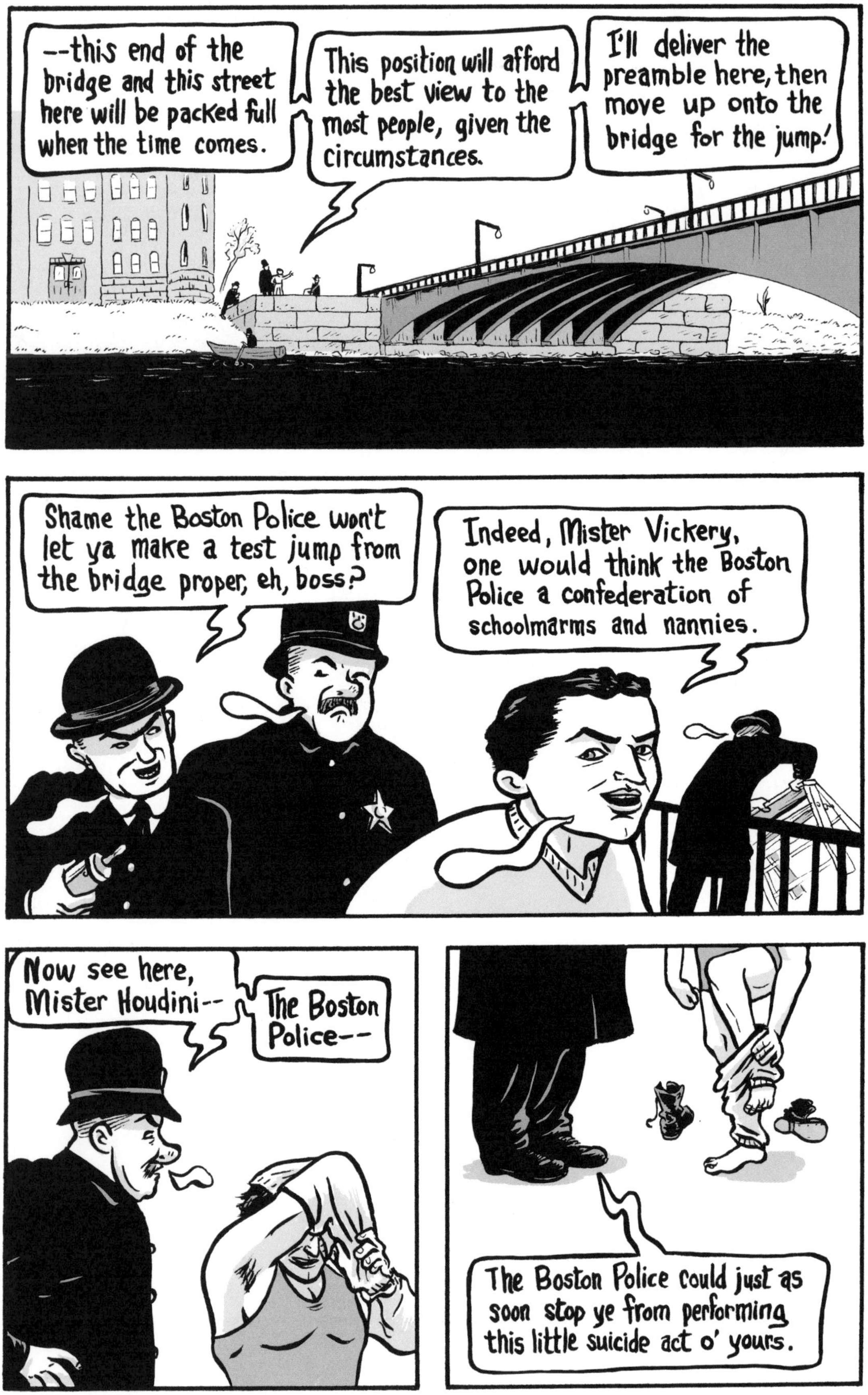
--this end of the bridge and this street here will be packed full when the time comes.
This position will afford the best view to the most people, given the circumstances.
I'll deliver the preamble here, then move up onto the bridge for the jump!
Shame the Boston Police won't let ya make a test jump from the bridge proper, eh, boss?
Indeed, Mister Vickery, one would think the Boston Police a confederation of schoolmarms and nannies.
Now see here, Mister Houdini--
The Boston Police--
The Boston Police could just as soon stop ye from performing this little suicide act o' yours.

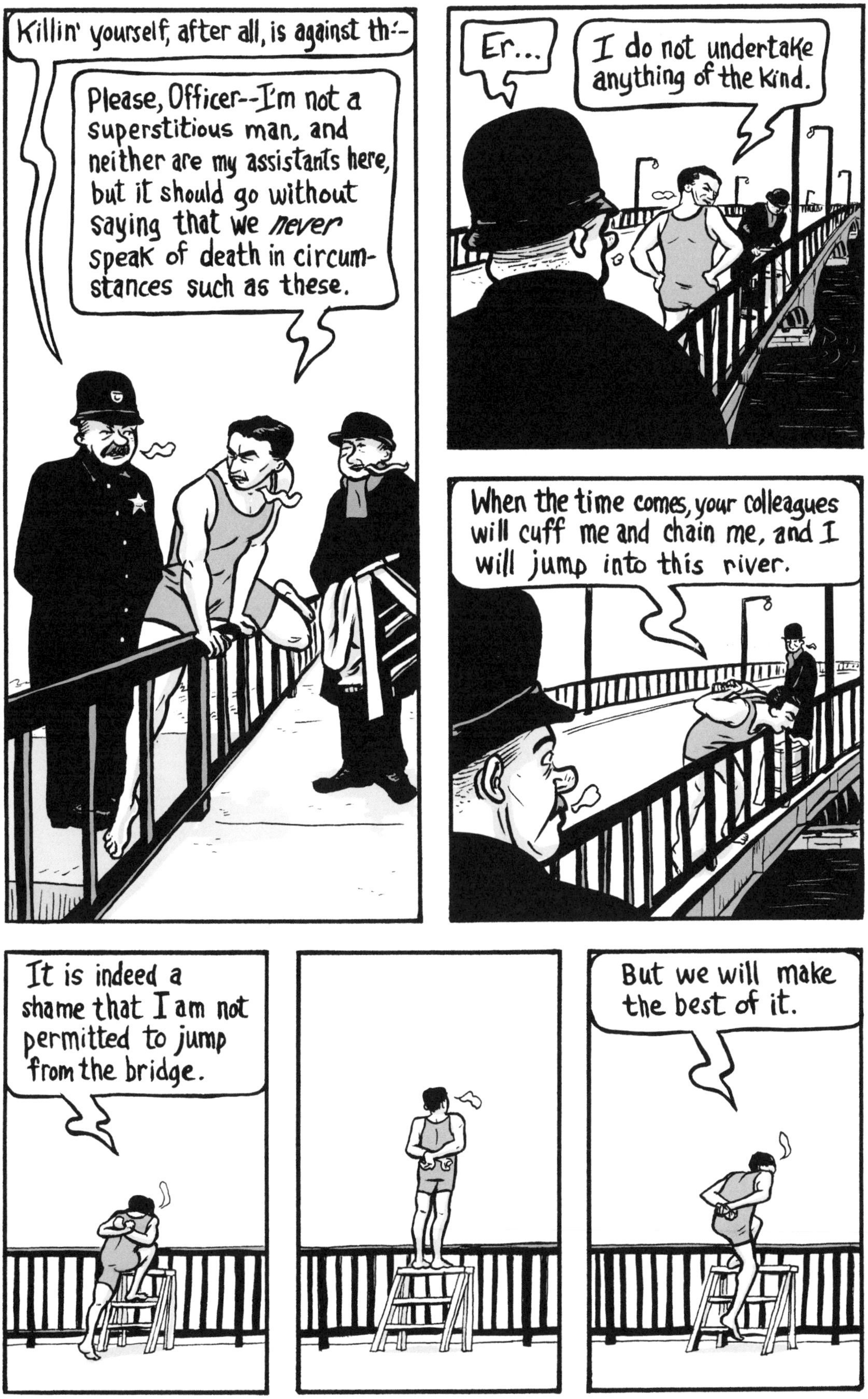
Killin' yourself, after all, is against th:-
Please, Officer--I'm not a superstitious man, and neither are my assistants here, but it should go without saying that we *never* speak of death in circumstances such as these.
Er...
I do not undertake anything of the kind.
When the time comes, your colleagues will cuff me and chain me, and I will jump into this river.
It is indeed a shame that I am not permitted to jump from the bridge.
But we will make the best of it.

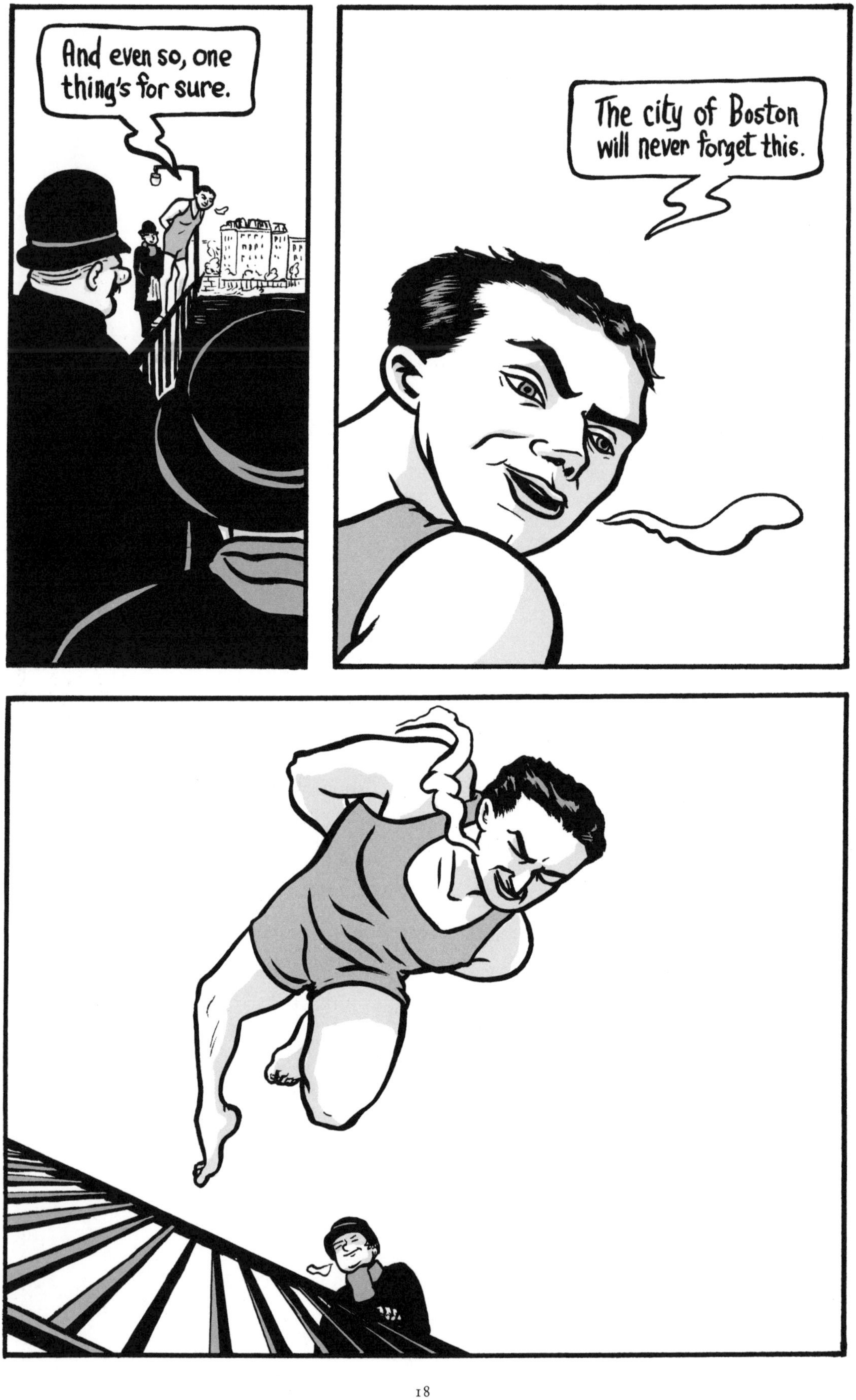
And even so, one thing's for sure.
The city of Boston will never forget this.

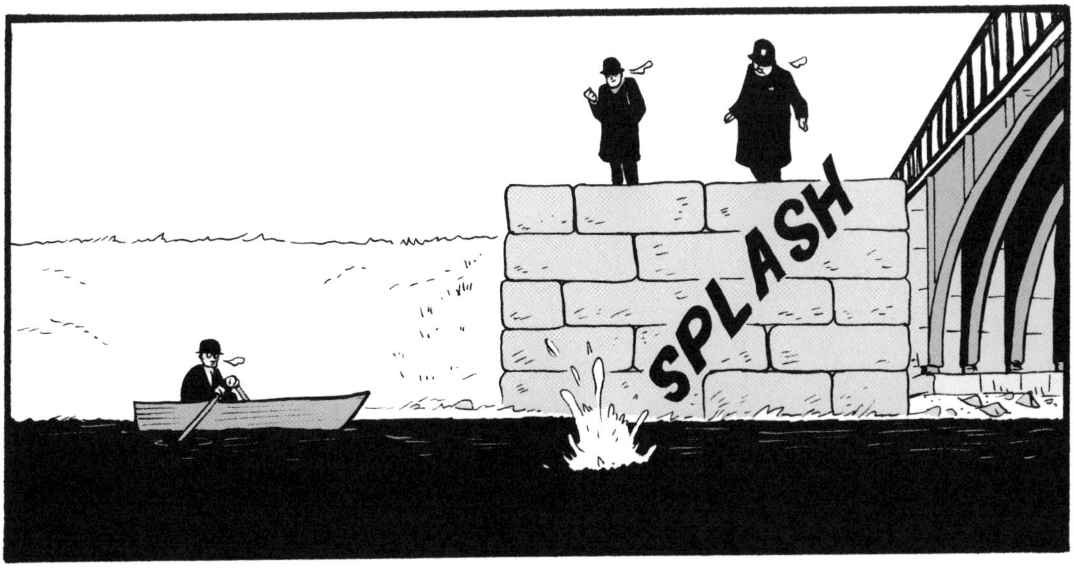
SPLASH

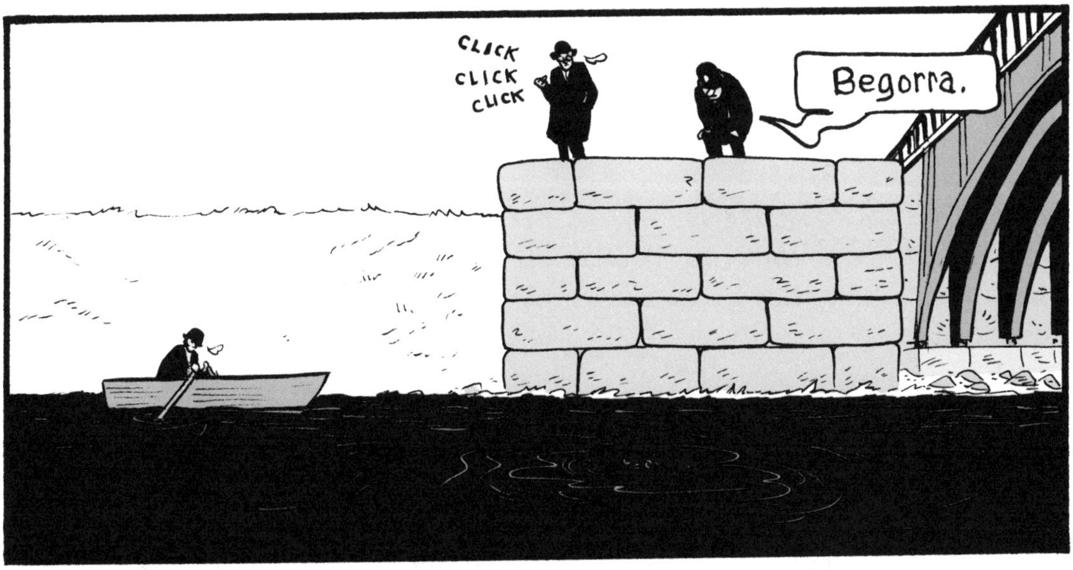
CLICK
CLICK
CLICK
Begorra.

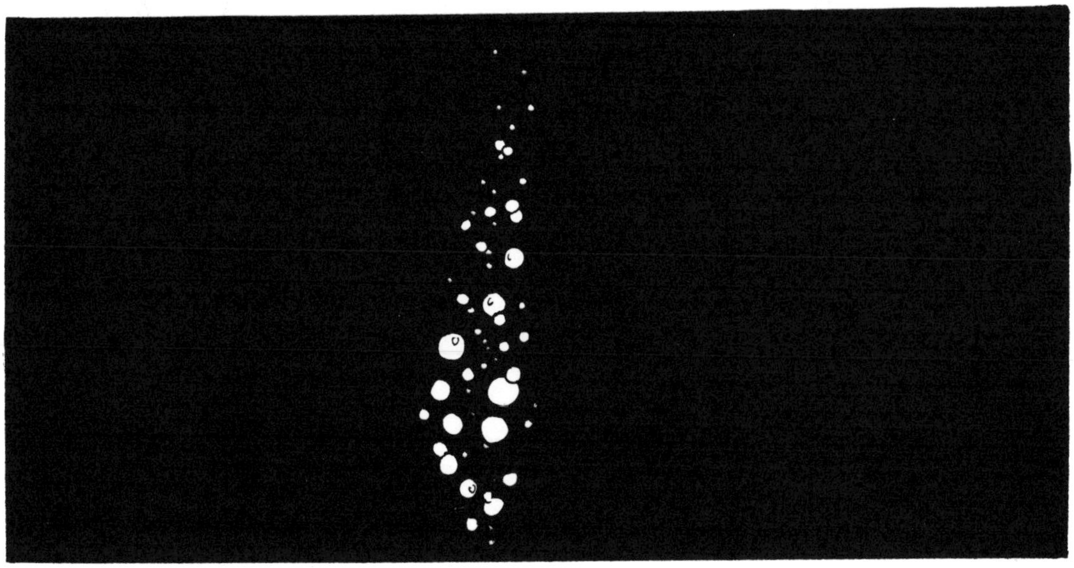

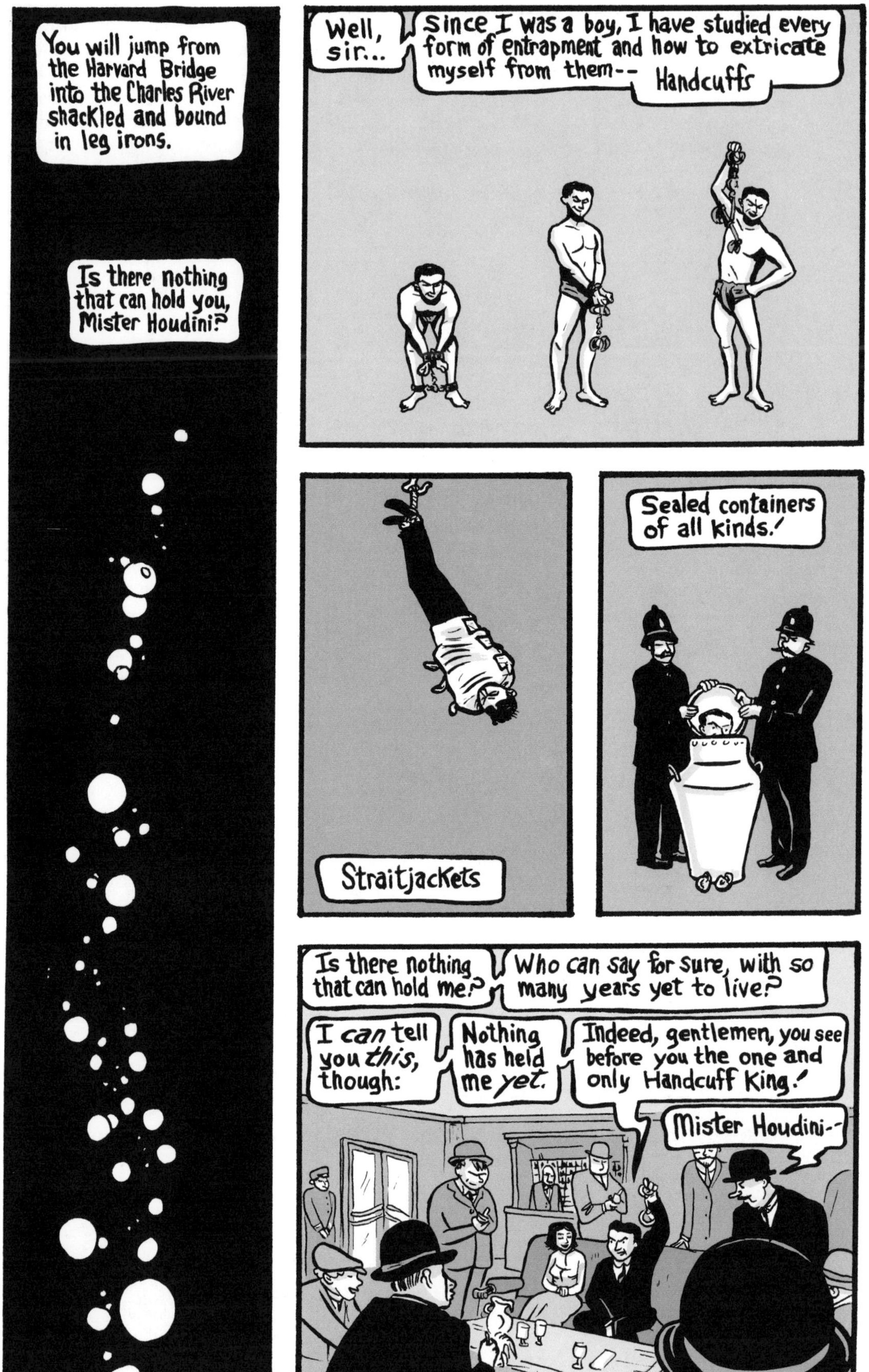
You will jump from the Harvard Bridge into the Charles River shackled and bound in leg irons.
Is there nothing that can hold you, Mister Houdini?
Well, sir...
Since I was a boy, I have studied every form of entrapment and how to extricate myself from them--
Handcuffs
Straitjackets
Sealed containers of all kinds!
Is there nothing that can hold me?
Who can say for sure, with so many years yet to live?
I *can* tell you *this*, though:
Nothing has held me *yet*.
Indeed, gentlemen, you see before you the one and only Handcuff King!
Mister Houdini--

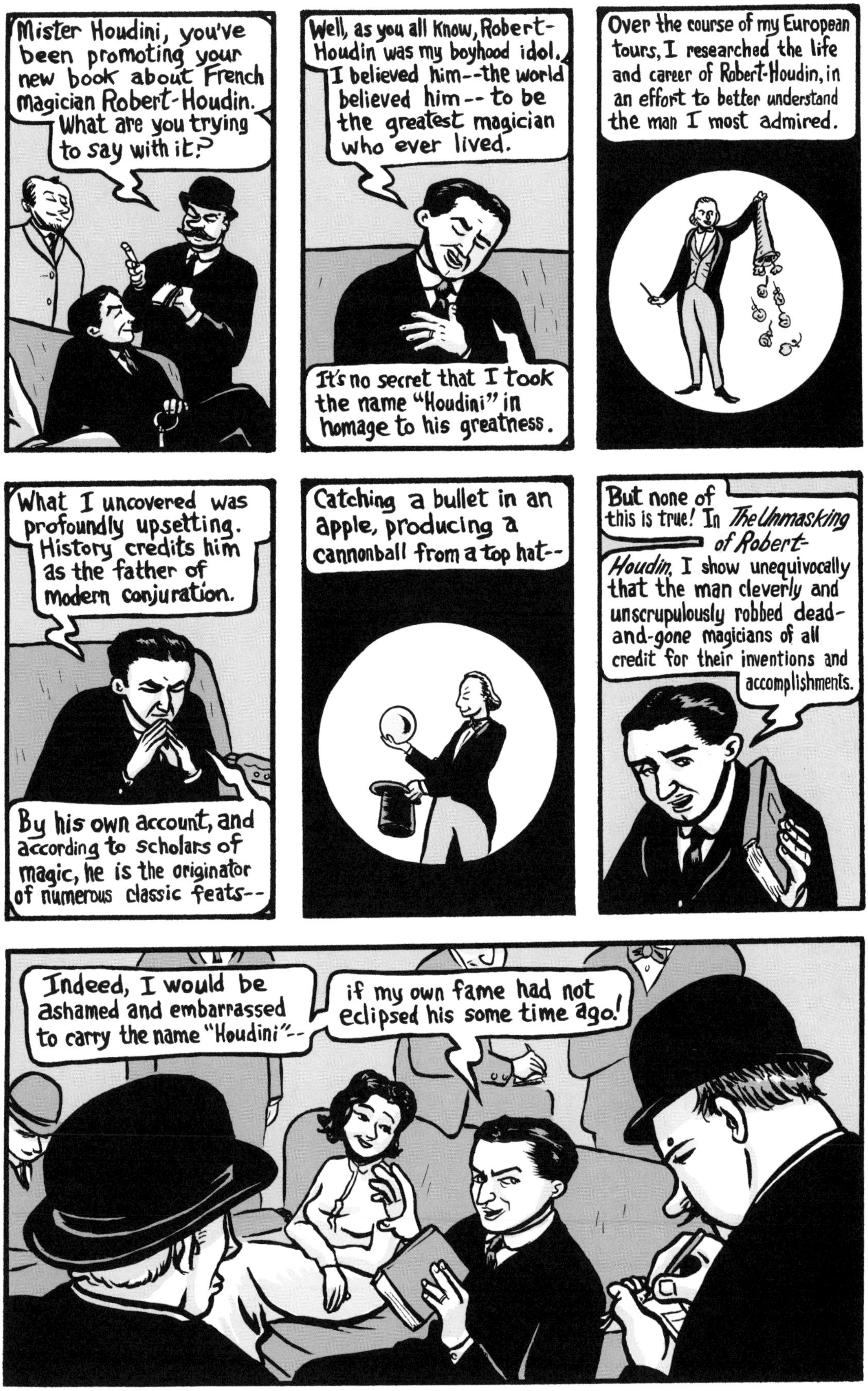
Mister Houdini, you've been promoting your new book about French magician Robert-Houdin.
What are you trying to say with it?
Well, as you all know, Robert-Houdin was my boyhood idol.
I believed him--the world believed him -- to be the greatest magician who ever lived.
It's no secret that I took the name "Houdini" in homage to his greatness.
Over the course of my European tours, I researched the life and career of Robert-Houdin, in an effort to better understand the man I most admired.
What I uncovered was profoundly upsetting.
History credits him as the father of modern conjuration.
By his own account, and according to scholars of magic, he is the originator of numerous classic feats--
Catching a bullet in an apple, producing a cannonball from a top hat--
But none of this is true! In *The Unmasking of Robert-Houdin*, I show unequivocally that the man cleverly and unscrupulously robbed dead-and-gone magicians of all credit for their inventions and accomplishments.
Indeed, I would be ashamed and embarrassed to carry the name "Houdini"--
if my own fame had not eclipsed his some time ago!

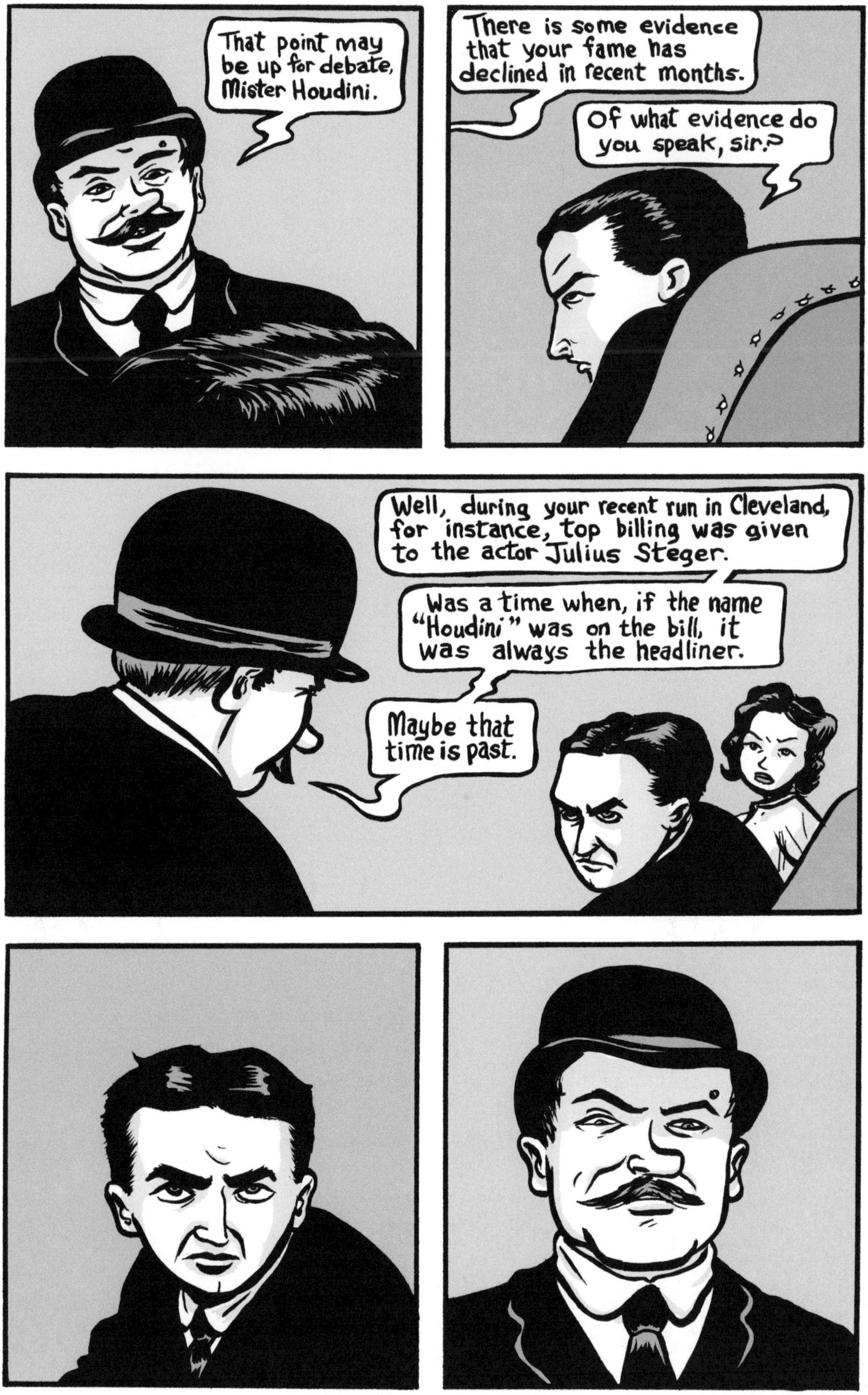
That point may be up for debate, Mister Houdini.
There is some evidence that your fame has declined in recent months.
Of what evidence do you speak, sir?
Well, during your recent run in Cleveland, for instance, top billing was given to the actor Julius Steger.
Was a time when, if the name "Houdini" was on the bill, it was always the headliner.
Maybe that time is past.

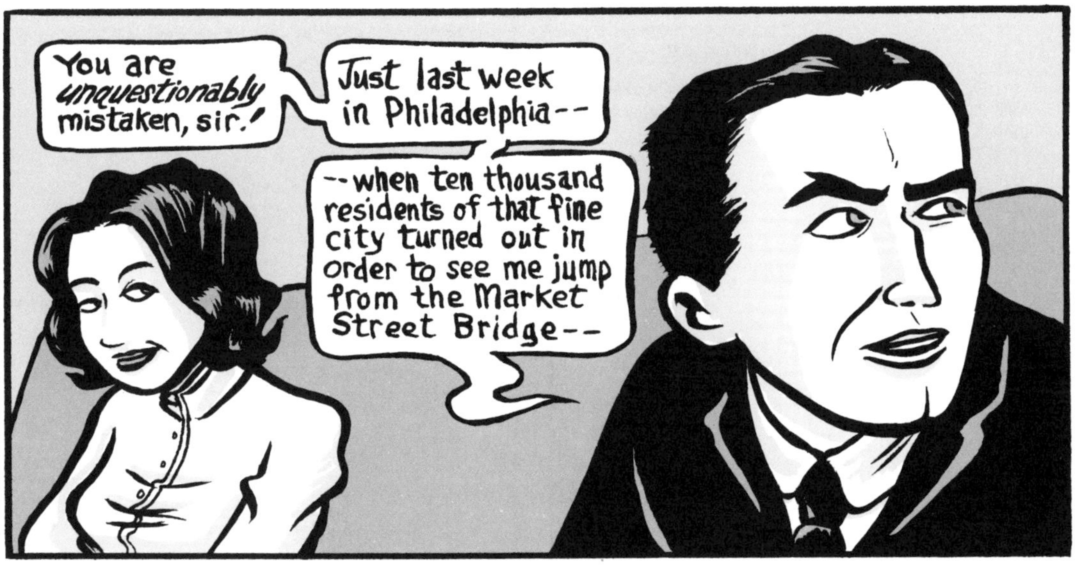
You are *unquestionably* mistaken, sir.!
Just last week in Philadelphia--
--when ten thousand residents of that fine city turned out in order to see me jump from the Market Street Bridge--

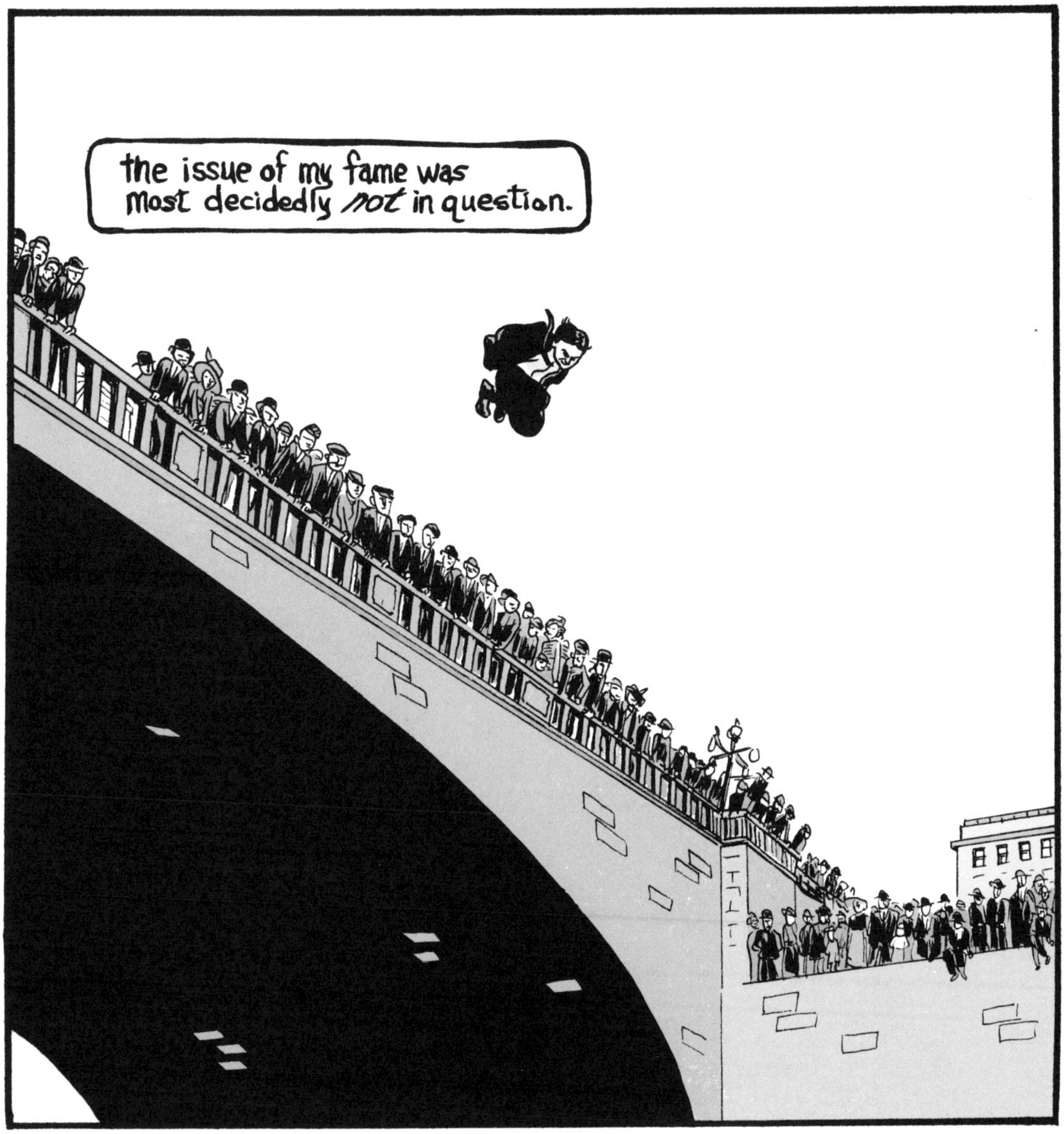
the issue of my fame was most decidedly *not* in question.

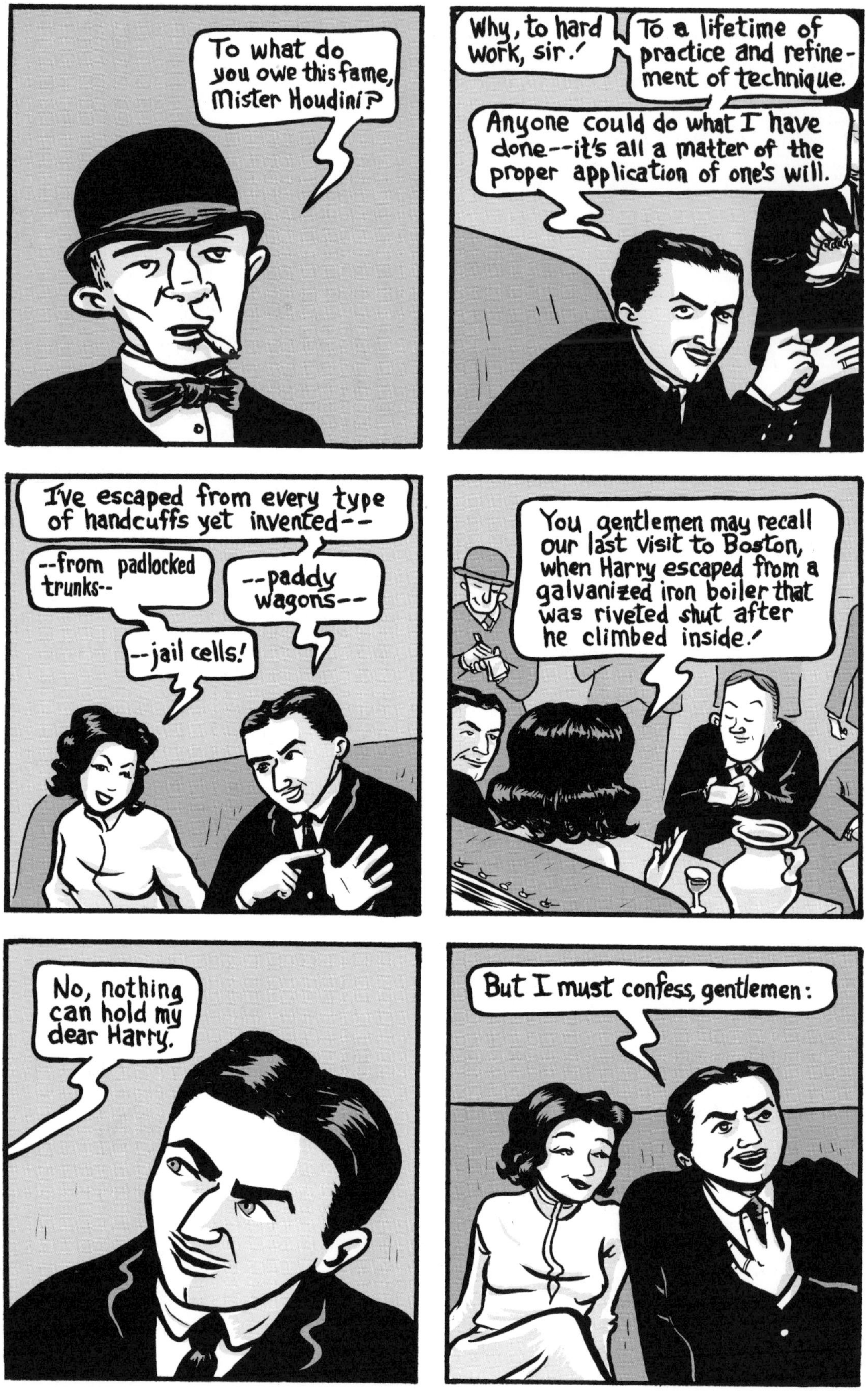
To what do you owe this fame, Mister Houdini?
Why, to hard work, sir!
To a lifetime of practice and refinement of technique.
Anyone could do what I have done--it's all a matter of the proper application of one's will.
I've escaped from every type of handcuffs yet invented--
--from padlocked trunks--
--paddy wagons--
--jail cells!
You gentlemen may recall our last visit to Boston, when Harry escaped from a galvanized iron boiler that was riveted shut after he climbed inside!
No, nothing can hold my dear Harry.
But I must confess, gentlemen:

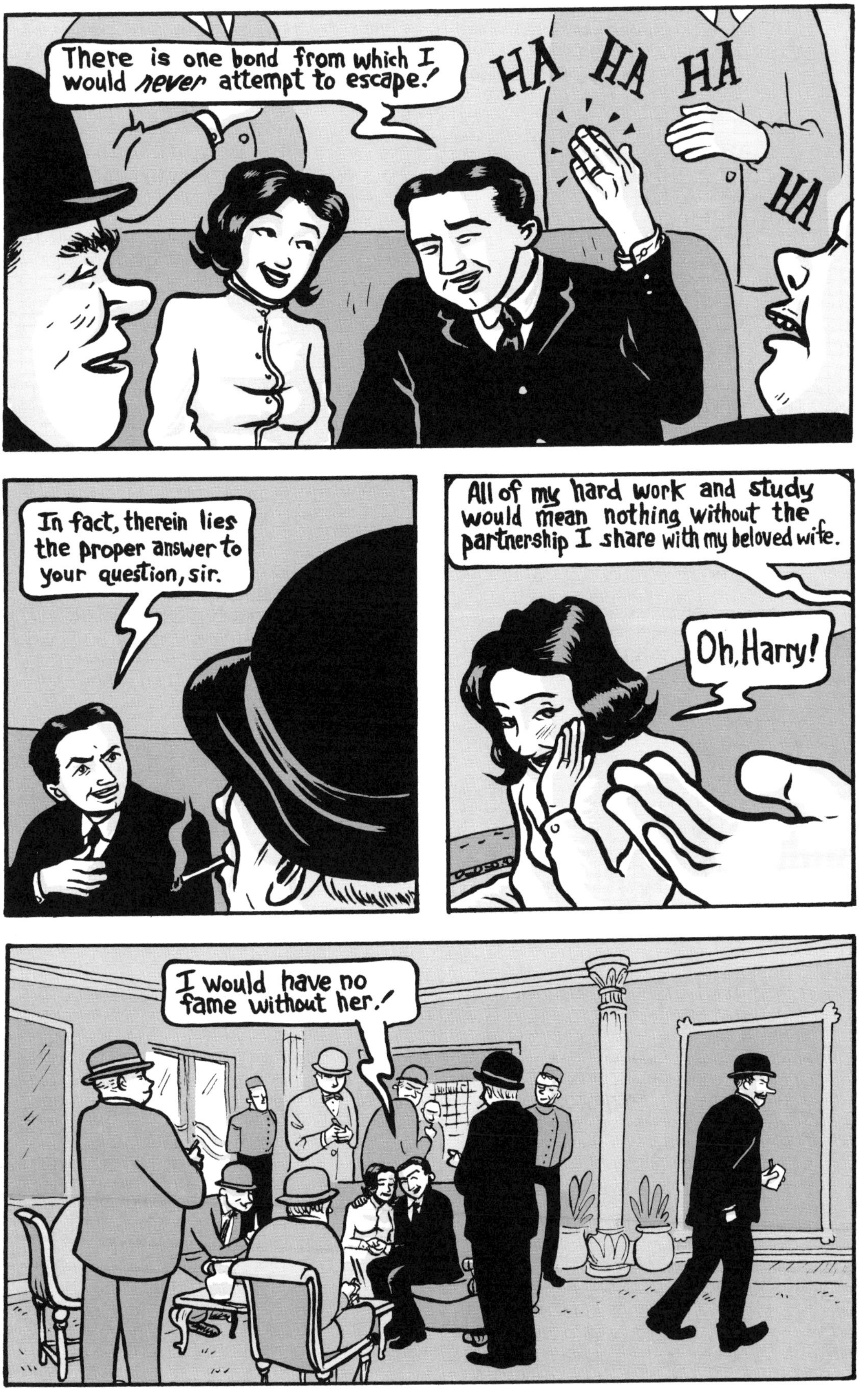

There is one bond from which I would *never* attempt to escape!
HA HA HA
HA
In fact, therein lies the proper answer to your question, sir.
All of my hard work and study would mean nothing without the partnership I share with my beloved wife.
Oh, Harry!
I would have no fame without her!

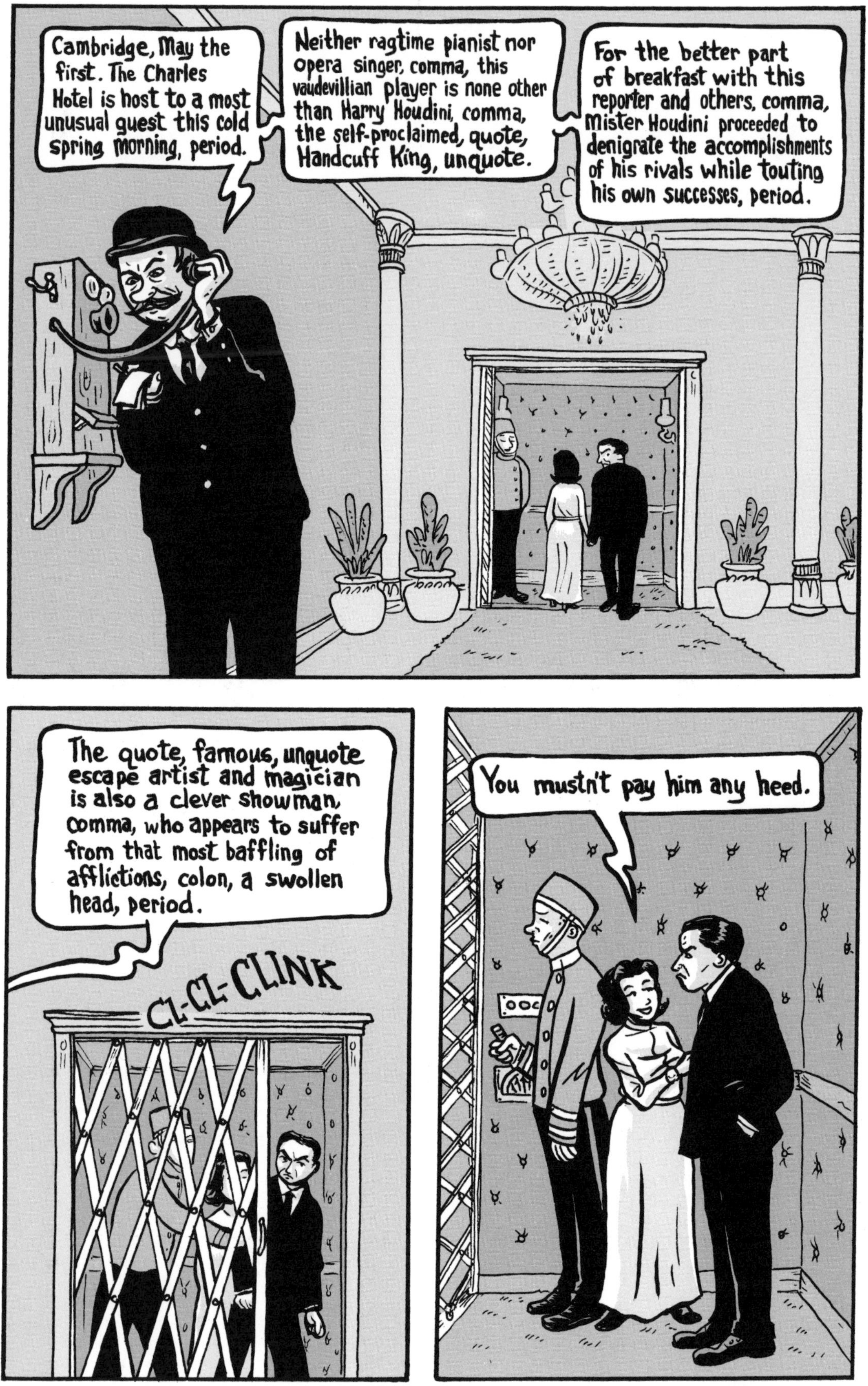
Cambridge, May the first. The Charles Hotel is host to a most unusual guest this cold spring morning, period.
Neither ragtime pianist nor opera singer, comma, this vaudevillian player is none other than Harry Houdini, comma, the self-proclaimed, quote, Handcuff King, unquote.
For the better part of breakfast with this reporter and others, comma, Mister Houdini proceeded to denigrate the accomplishments of his rivals while touting his own successes, period.
The quote, famous, unquote escape artist and magician is also a clever showman, comma, who appears to suffer from that most baffling of afflictions, colon, a swollen head, period.
CL-CL-CLINK
You mustn't pay him any heed.

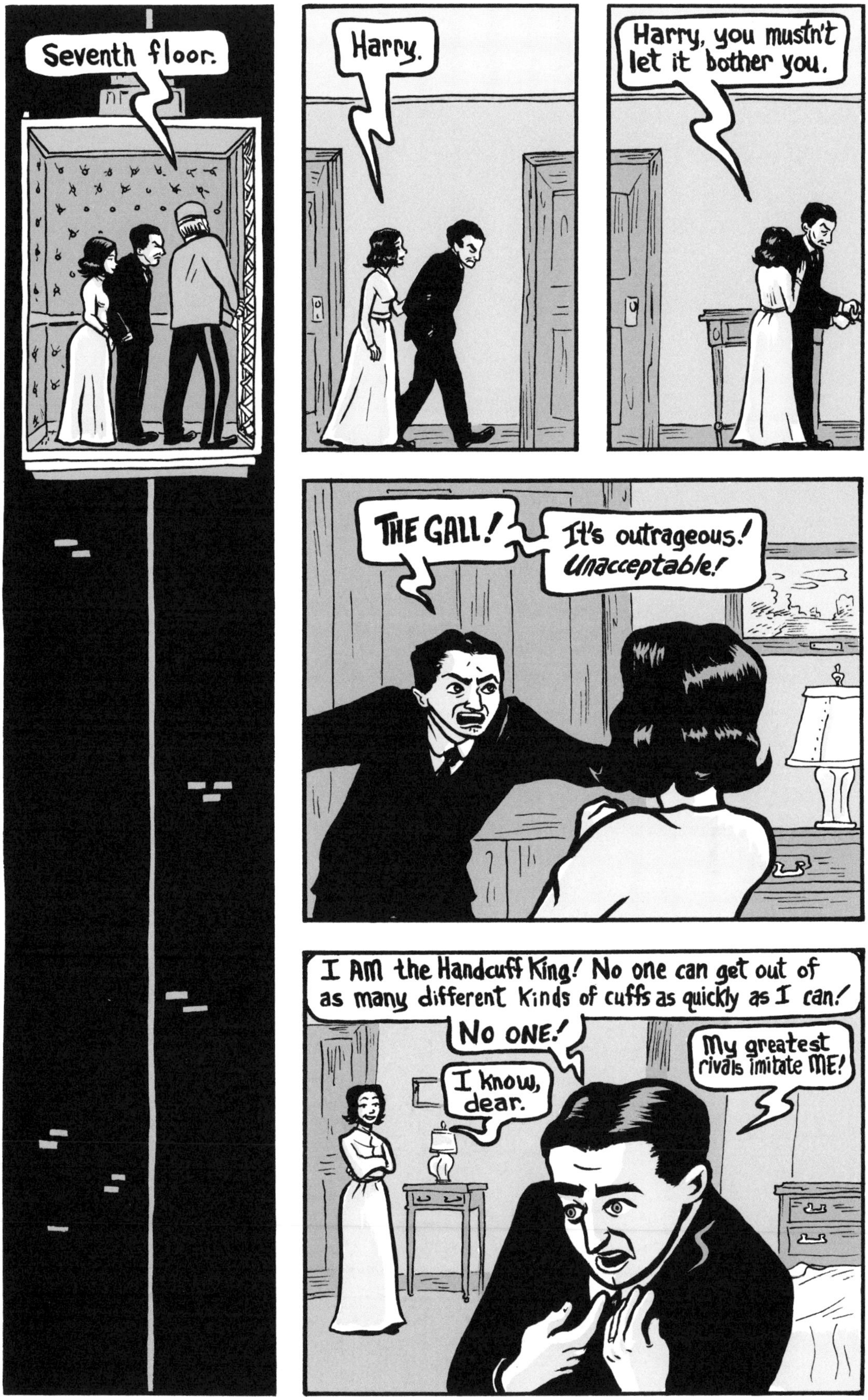
Seventh floor.
Harry.
Harry, you mustn't let it bother you.
THE GALL!
It's outrageous! Unacceptable!
I AM the Handcuff King! No one can get out of as many different kinds of cuffs as quickly as I can!
NO ONE!
I know, dear.
My greatest rivals imitate ME!

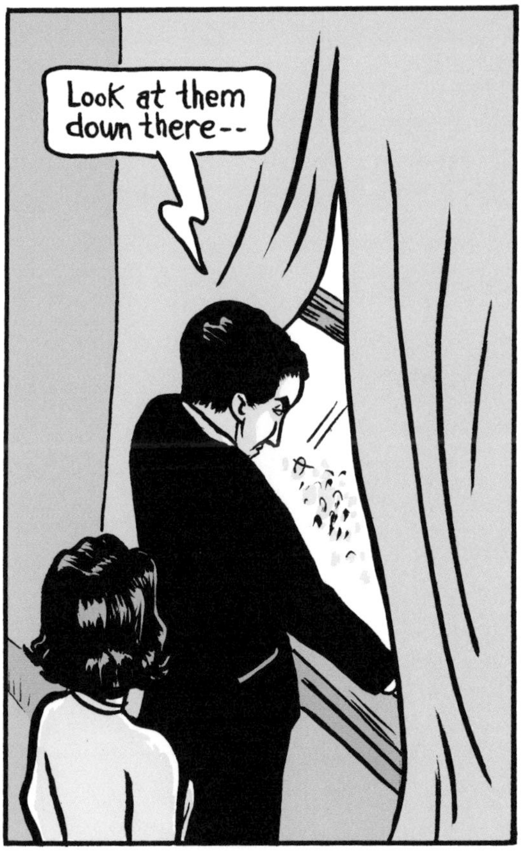
Look at them down there--

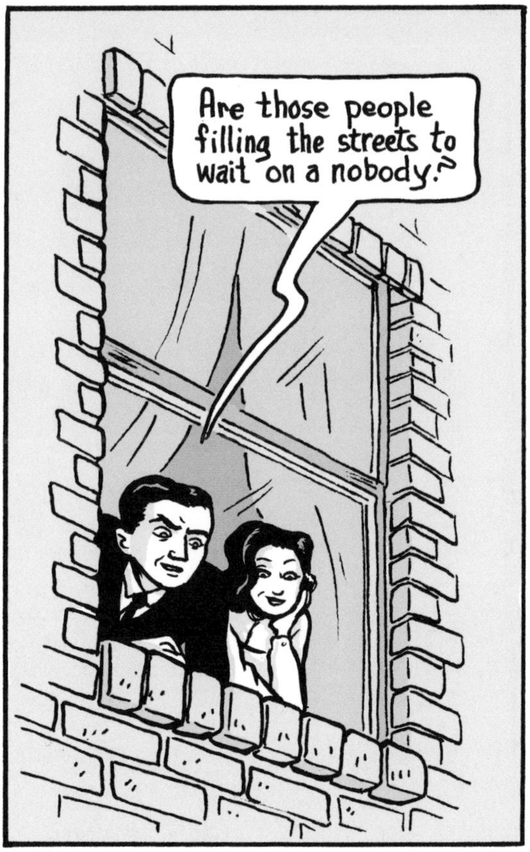
Are those people filling the streets to wait on a nobody?

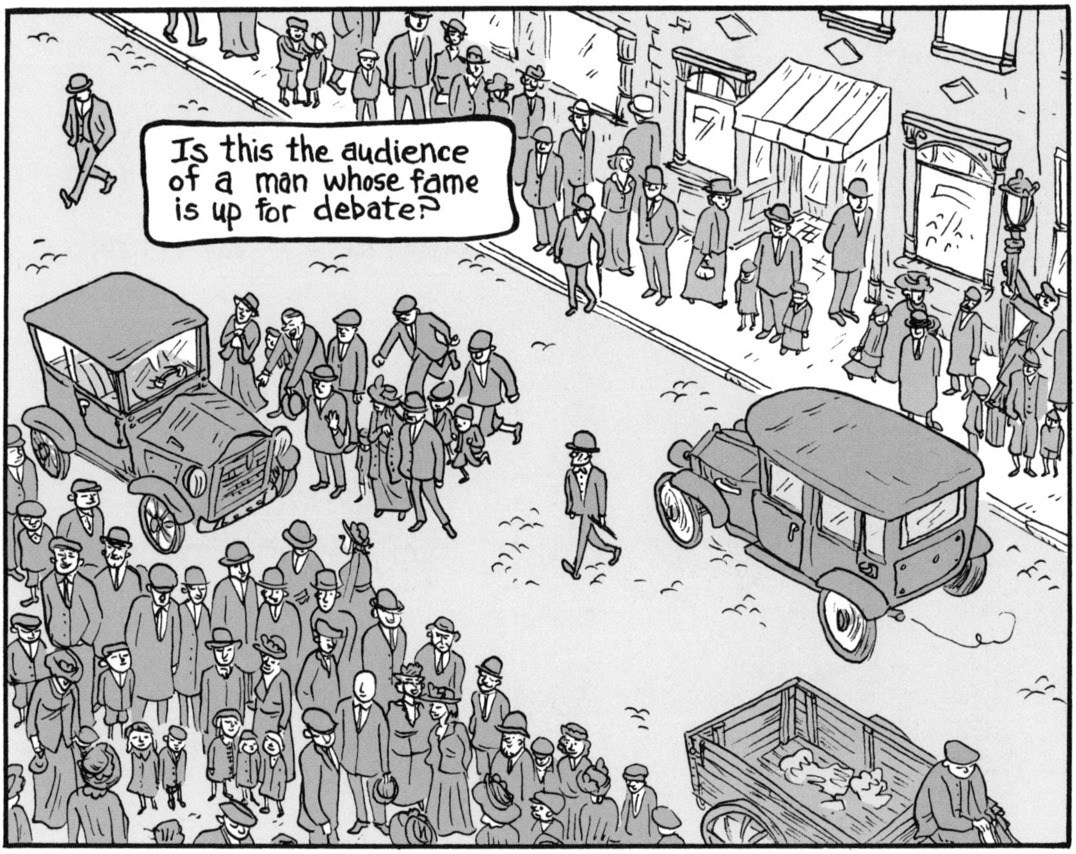
Is this the audience of a man whose fame is up for debate?

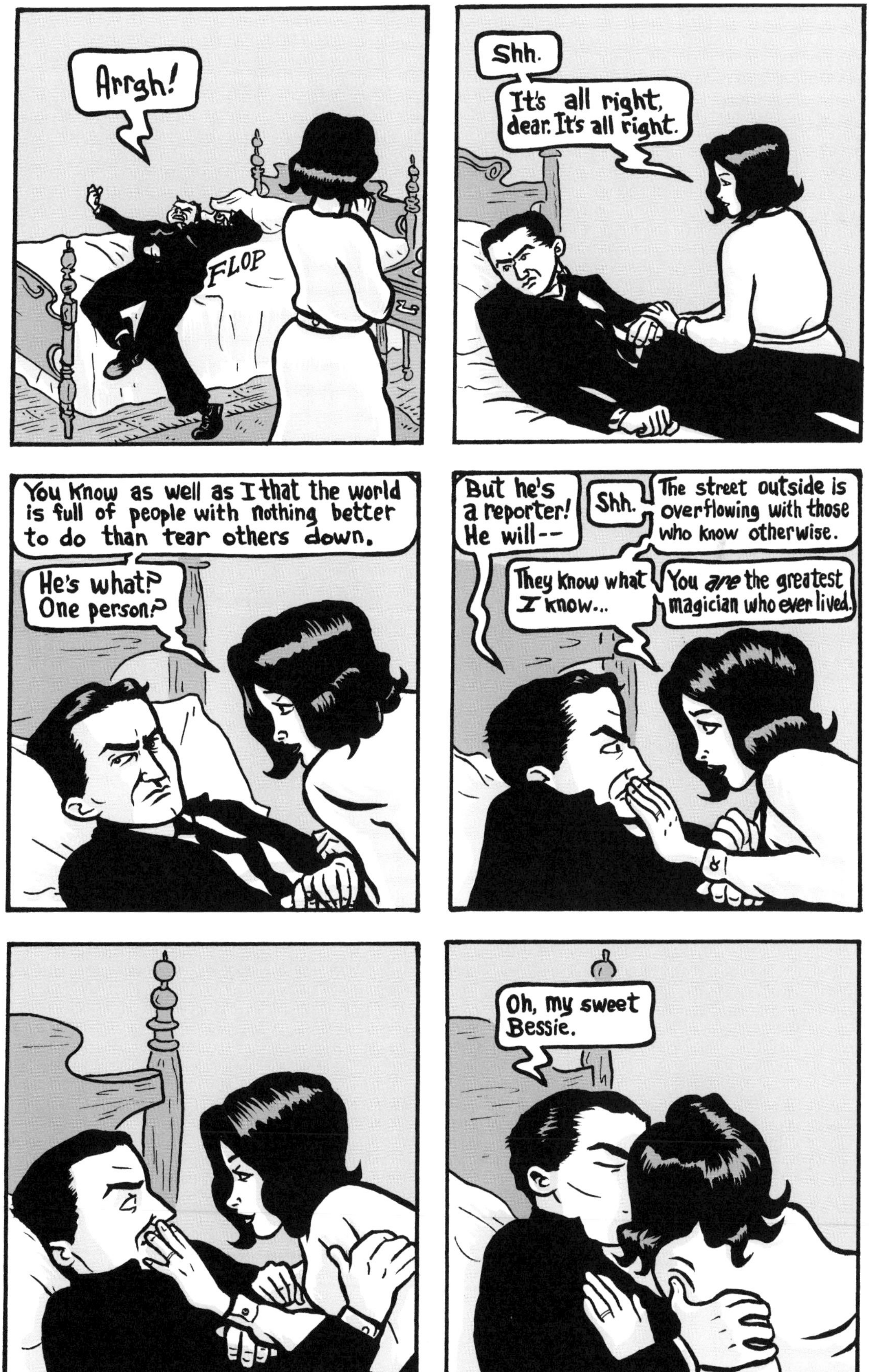

Arrgh!
FLOP
Shh.
It's all right, dear. It's all right.
You know as well as I that the world is full of people with nothing better to do than tear others down.
He's what? One person?
But he's a reporter! He will--
Shh.
The street outside is overflowing with those who know otherwise.
They know what I know...
You are the greatest magician who ever lived.
Oh, my sweet Bessie.

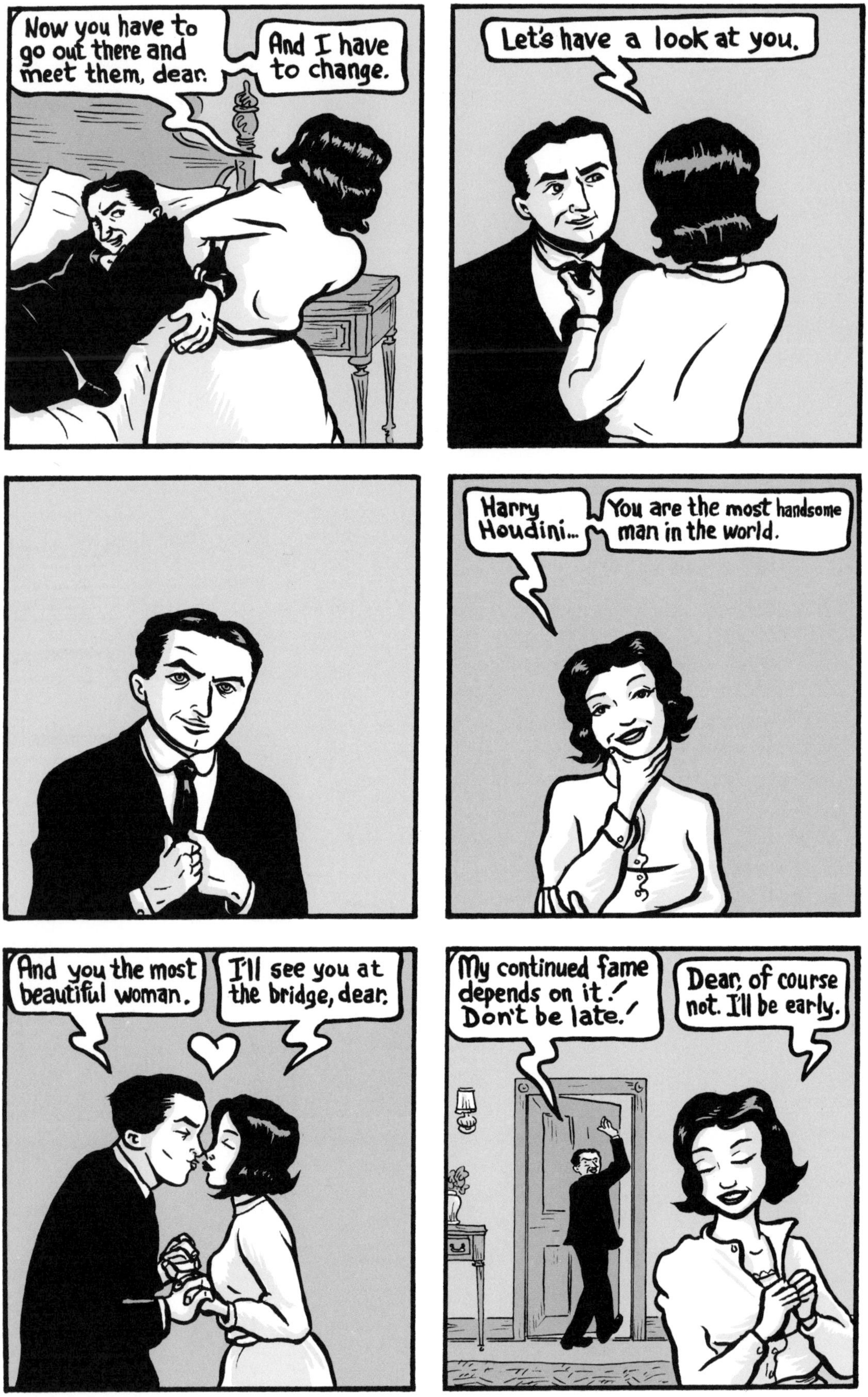
Now you have to go out there and meet them, dear.
And I have to change.
Let's have a look at you.
Harry Houdini...
You are the most handsome man in the world.
And you the most beautiful woman.
I'll see you at the bridge, dear.
My continued fame depends on it! Don't be late!
Dear, of course not. I'll be early.

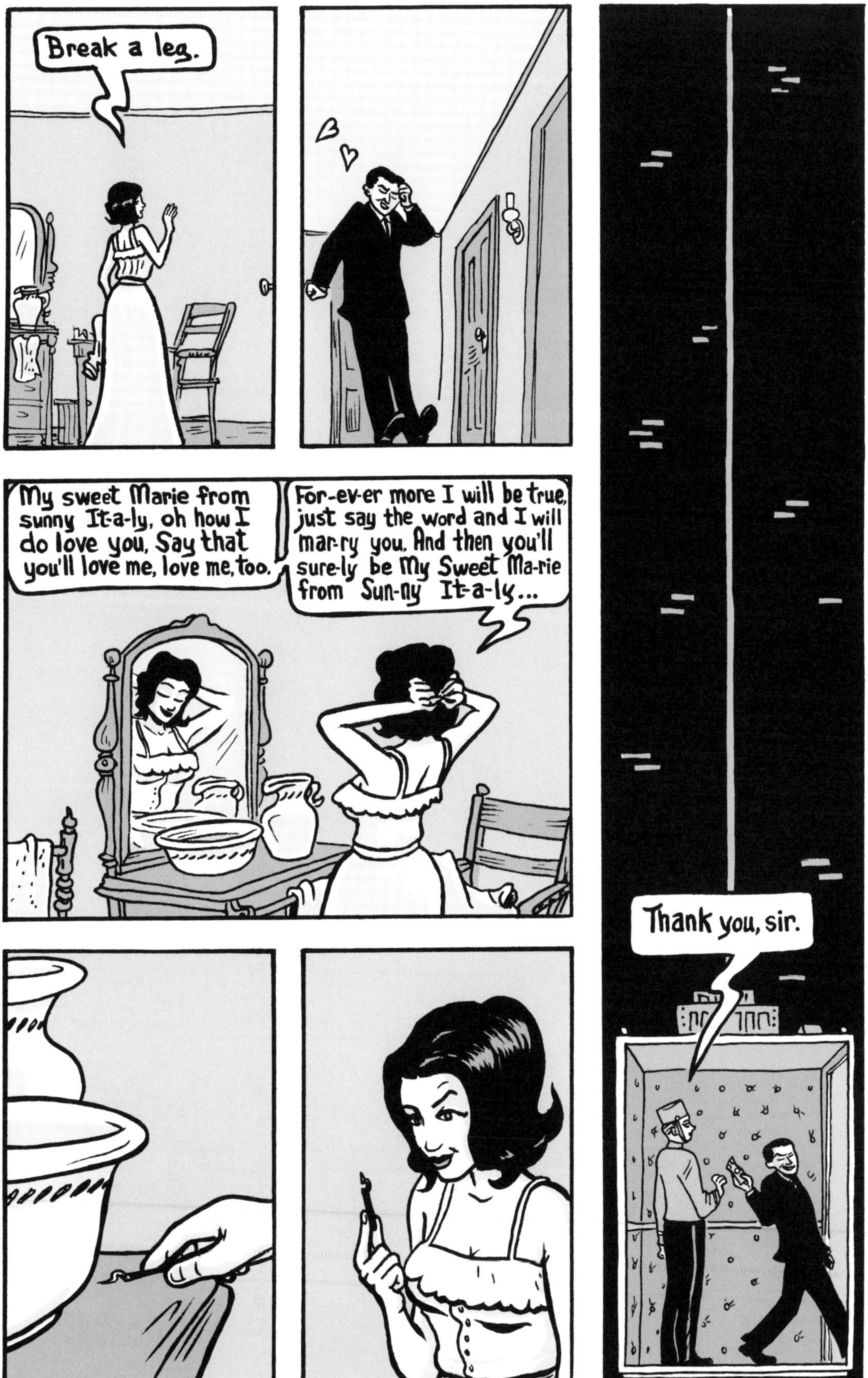

Break a leg.
My sweet Marie from sunny It-a-ly, oh how I do love you, Say that you'll love me, love me, too.
For-ev-er more I will be true, just say the word and I will mar-ry you. And then you'll sure-ly be My Sweet Ma-rie from Sun-ny It-a-ly...
Thank you, sir.

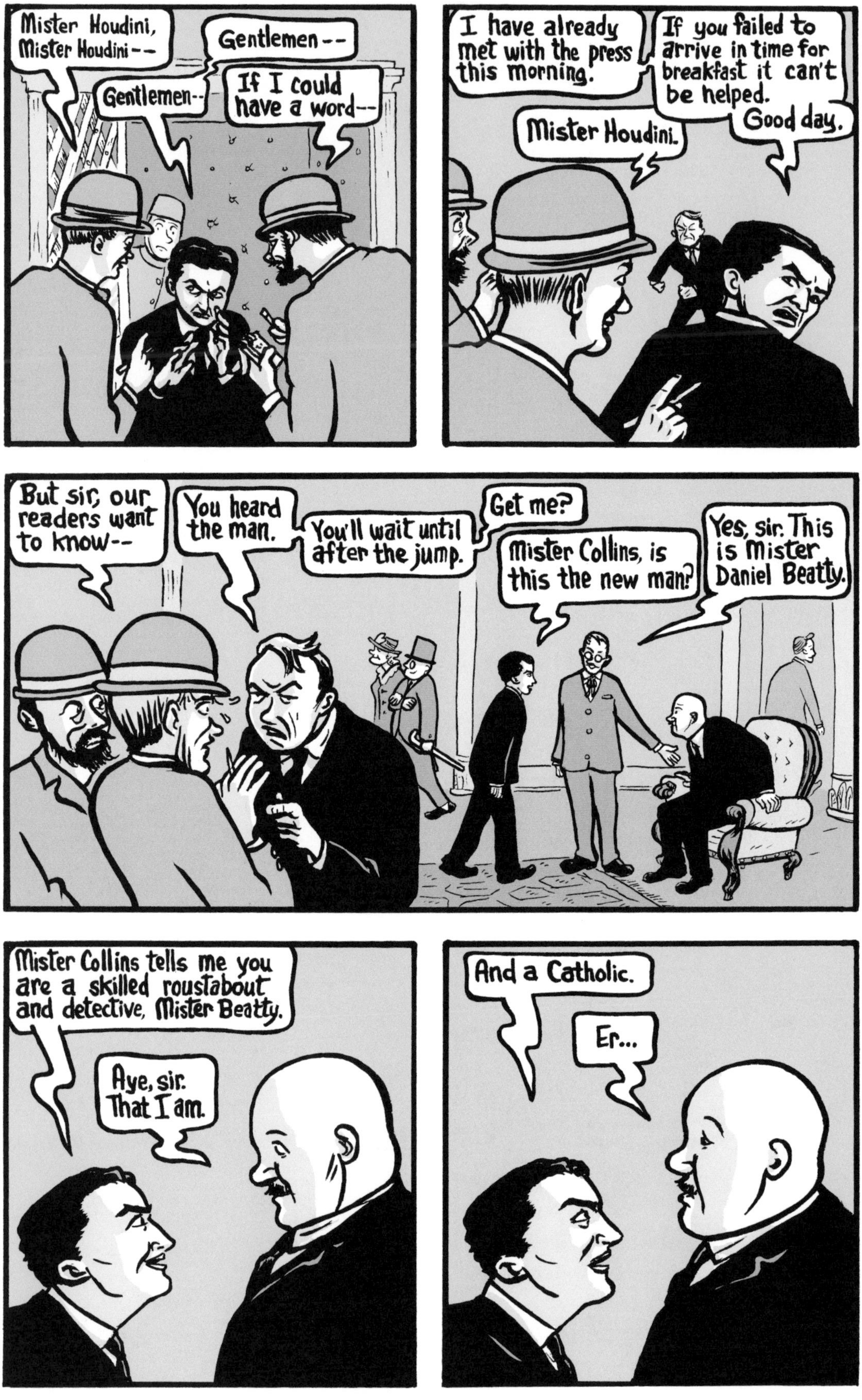
Mister Houdini, Mister Houdini--
Gentlemen--
Gentlemen--
If I could have a word--
I have already met with the press this morning.
Mister Houdini.
If you failed to arrive in time for breakfast it can't be helped.
Good day.
But sir, our readers want to know--
You heard the man.
You'll wait until after the jump.
Get me?
Mister Collins, is this the new man?
Yes, sir. This is Mister Daniel Beatty.
Mister Collins tells me you are a skilled roustabout and detective, Mister Beatty.
Aye, sir. That I am.
And a Catholic.
Er...

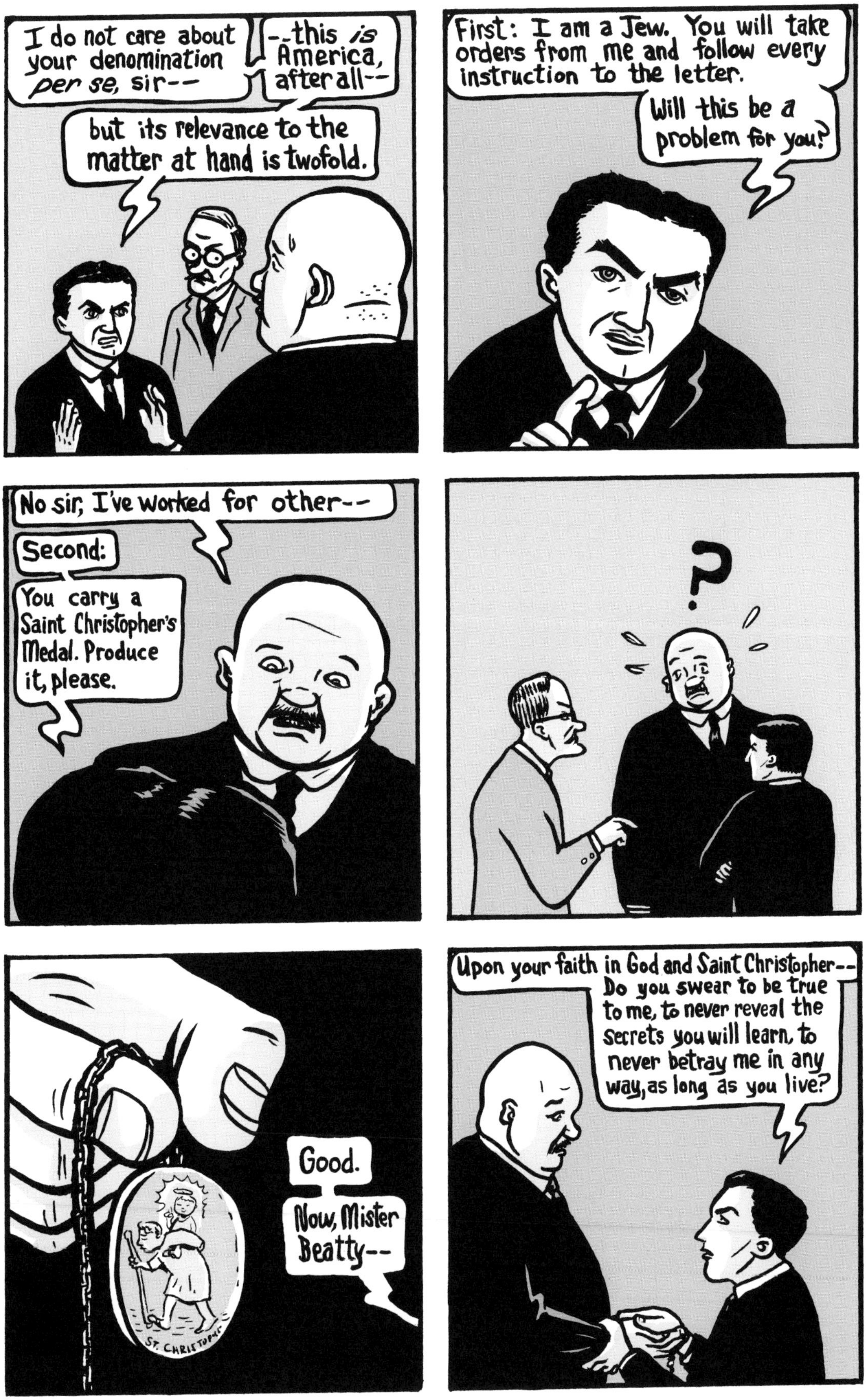
I do not care about your denomination *per se*, sir--
--this *is* America, after all--
but its relevance to the matter at hand is twofold.
First: I am a Jew. You will take orders from me and follow every instruction to the letter.
Will this be a problem for you?
No sir, I've worked for other--
Second:
You carry a Saint Christopher's Medal. Produce it, please.
?
ST. CHRISTOPHE
Good.
Now, Mister Beatty--
Upon your faith in God and Saint Christopher--
Do you swear to be true to me, to never reveal the secrets you will learn, to never betray me in any way, as long as you live?

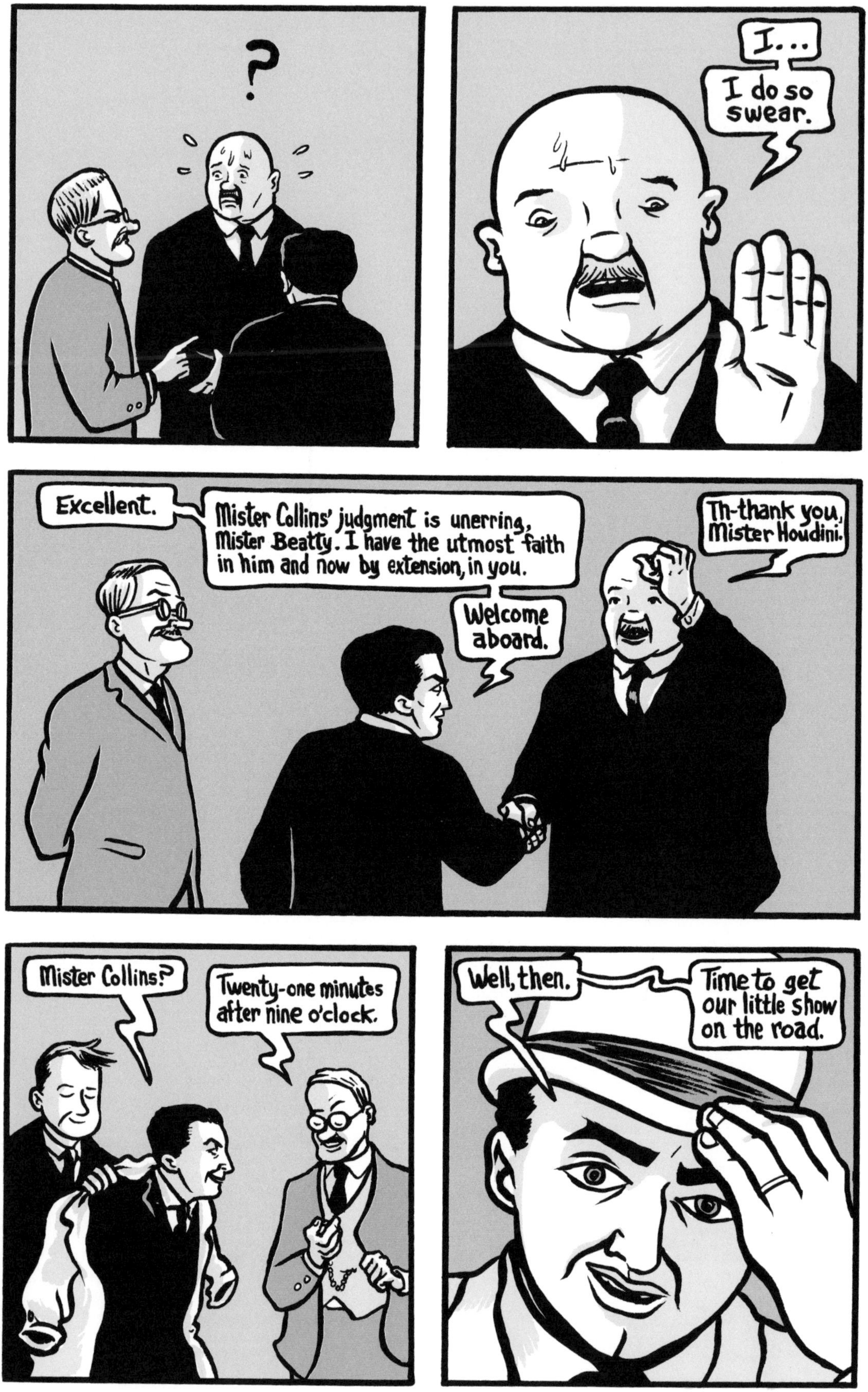
?
I...
I do so swear.
Excellent.
Mister Collins' judgment is unerring, Mister Beatty. I have the utmost faith in him and now by extension, in you.
Welcome aboard.
Th-thank you, Mister Houdini.
Mister Collins?
Twenty-one minutes after nine o'clock.
Well, then.
Time to get our little show on the road.

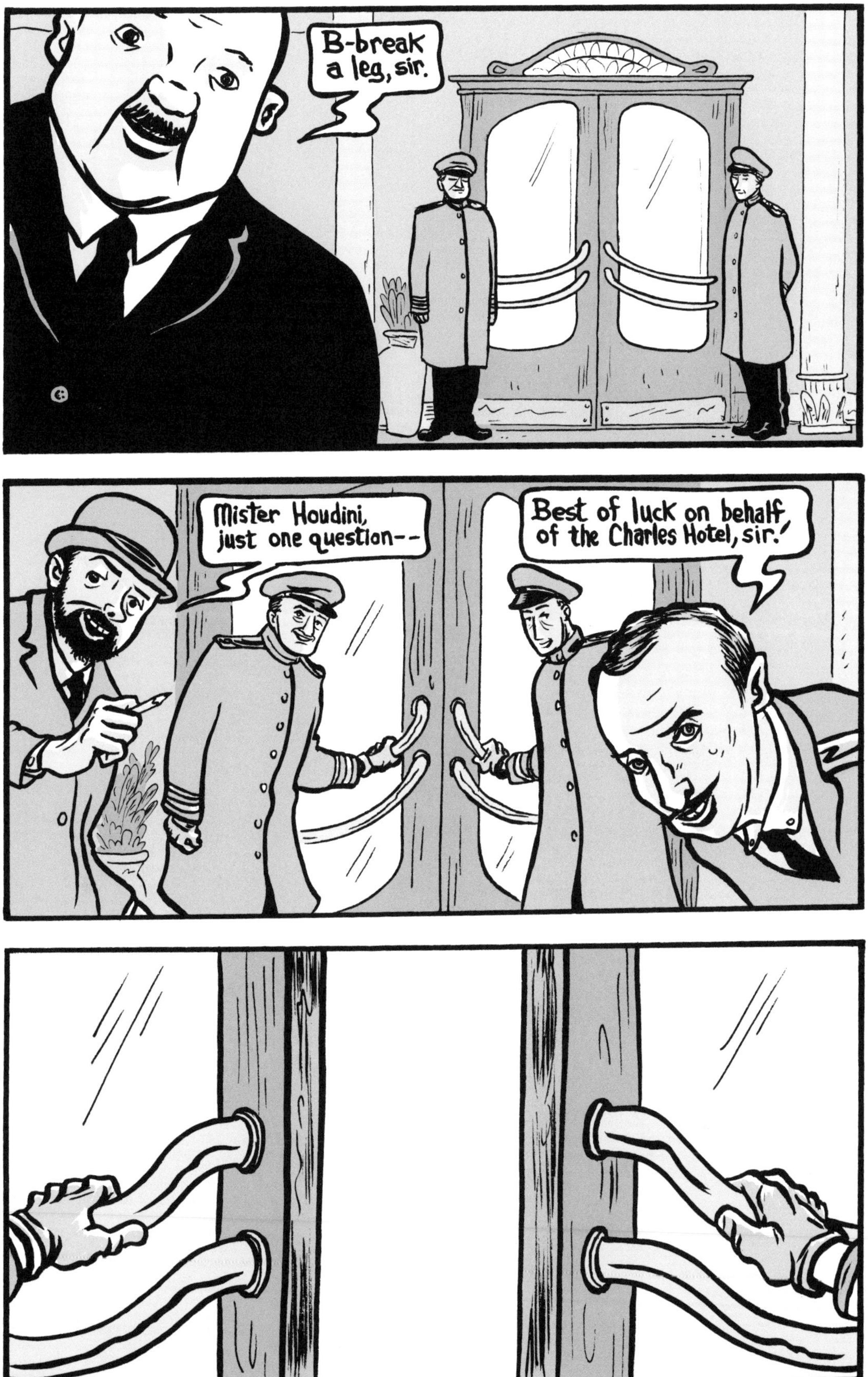
B-break a leg, sir.
Mister Houdini, just one question--
Best of luck on behalf of the Charles Hotel, sir.

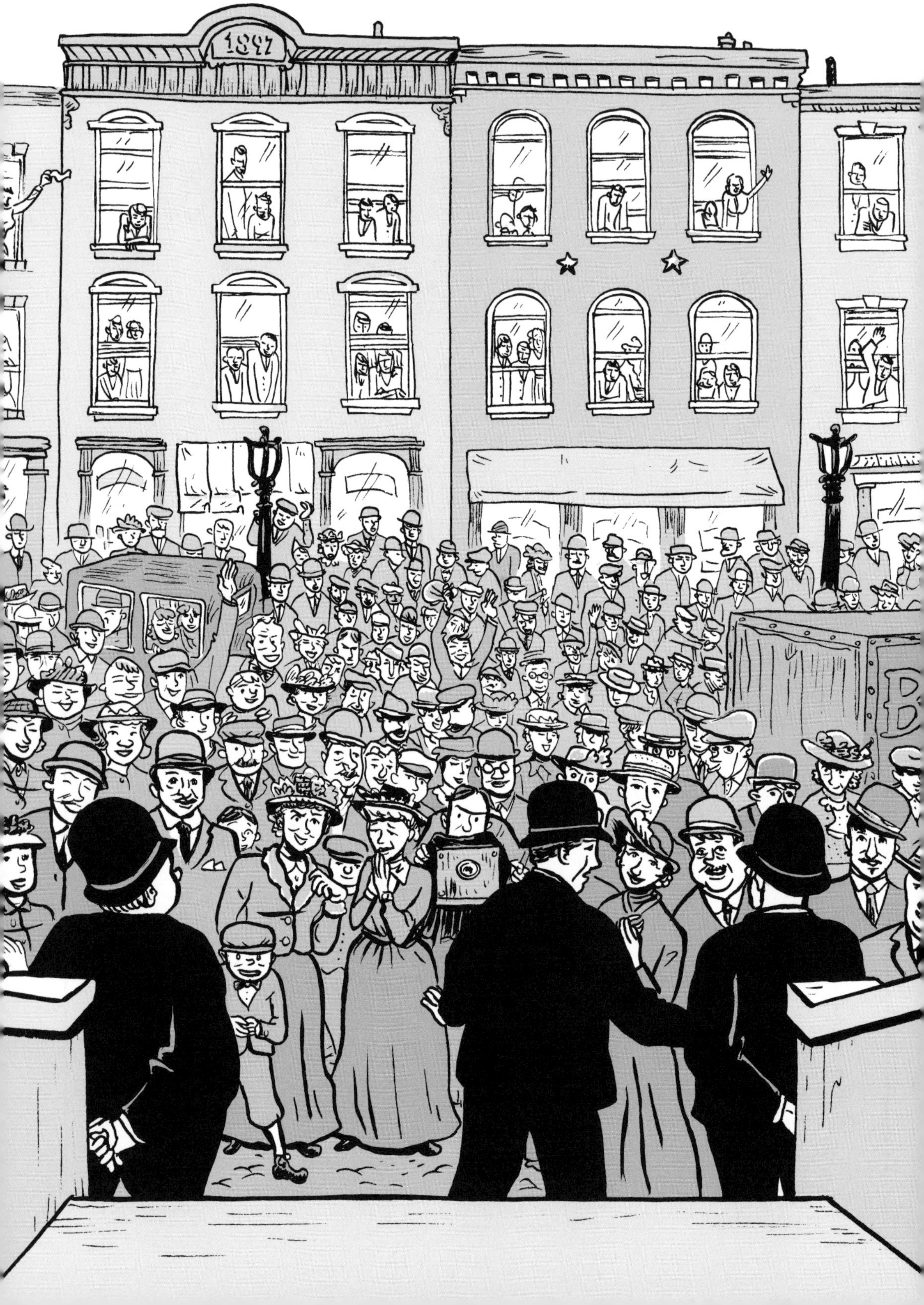
1847

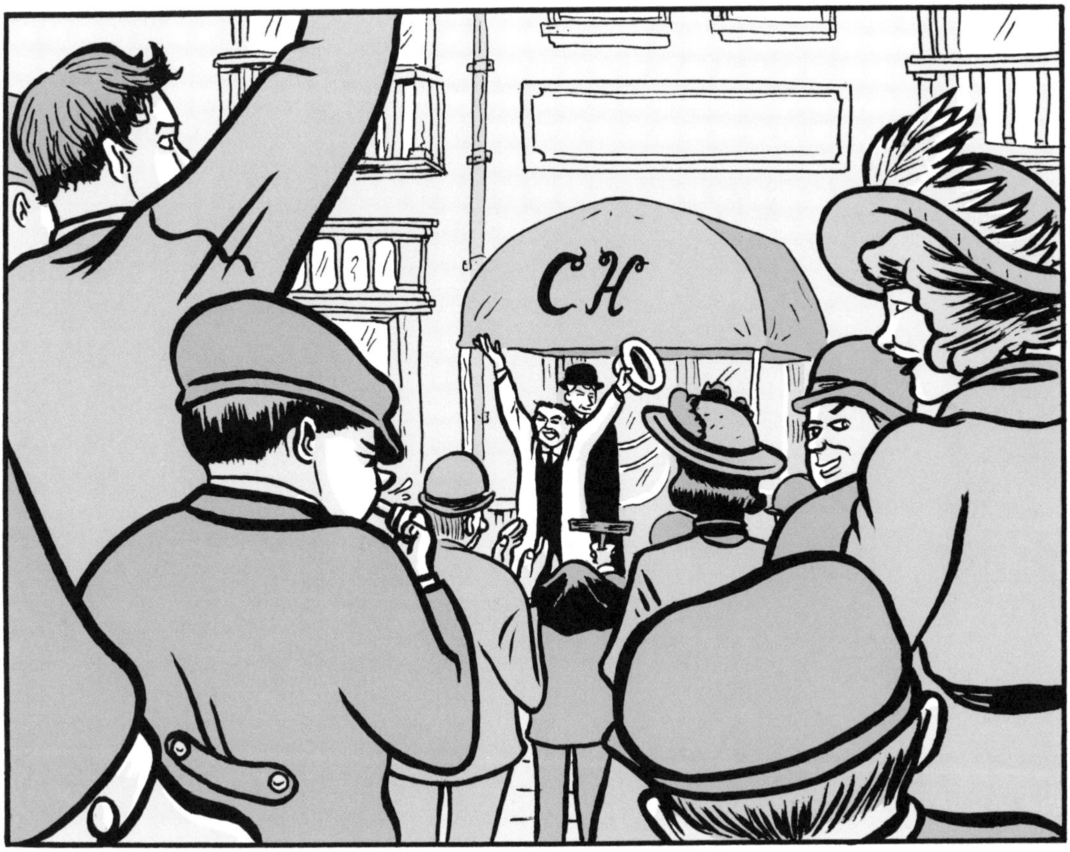
CH

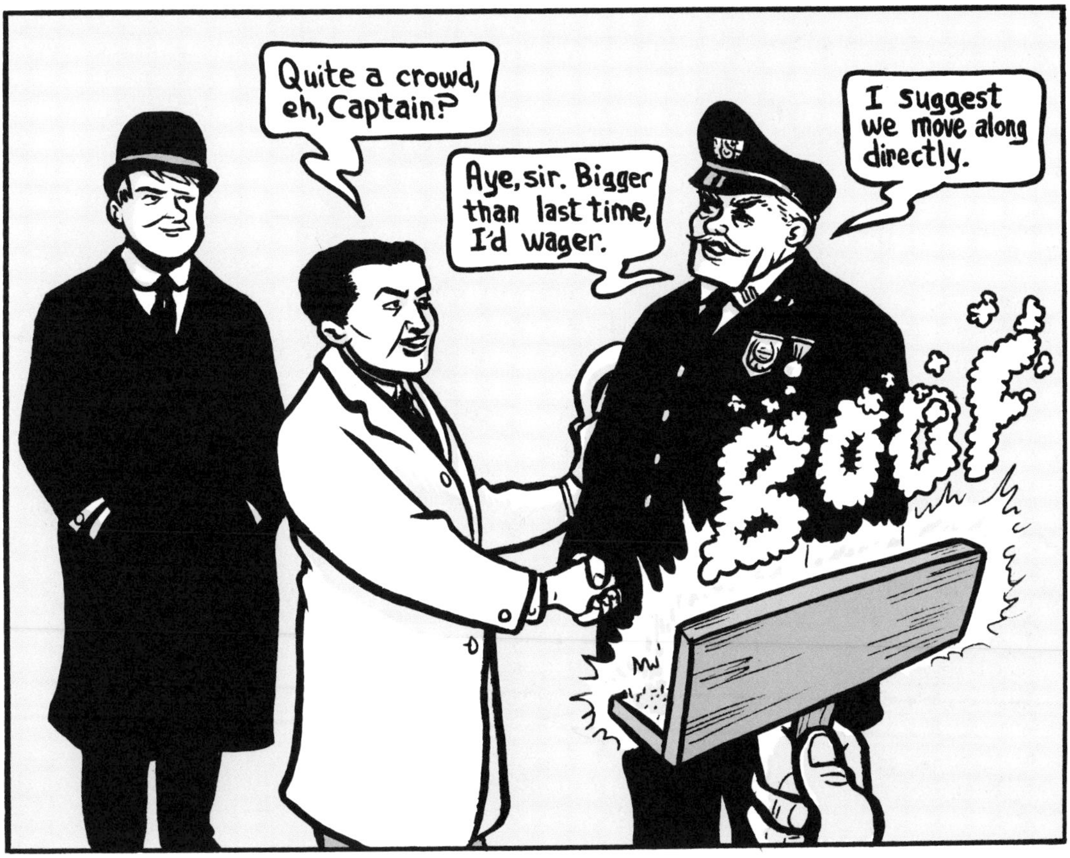
Quite a crowd, eh, Captain?
Aye, sir. Bigger than last time, I'd wager.
I suggest we move along directly.
BOOF

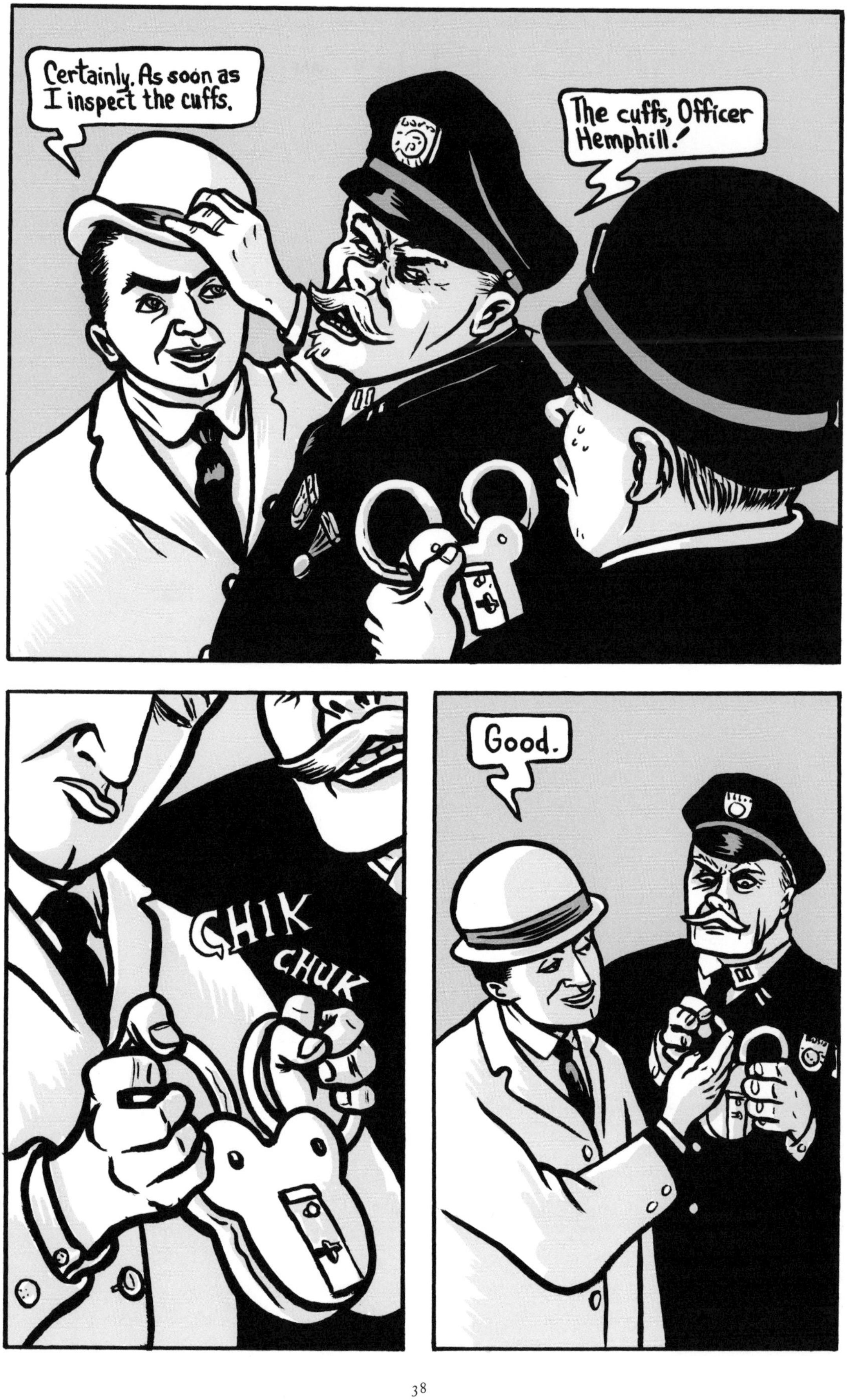
Certainly. As soon as I inspect the cuffs.
The cuffs, Officer Hemphill!
CHIK
CHUK
Good.

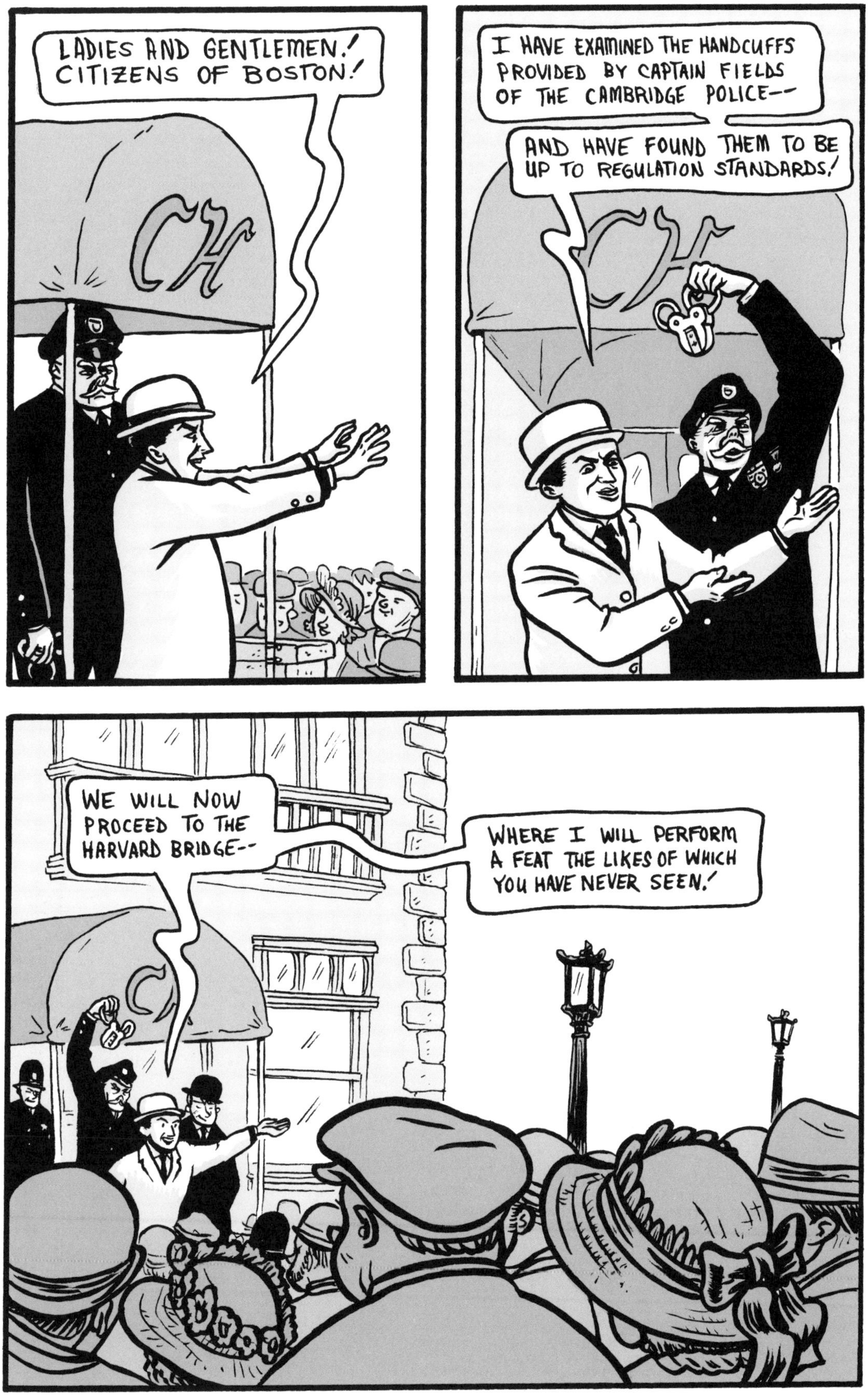
LADIES AND GENTLEMEN! CITIZENS OF BOSTON!
I HAVE EXAMINED THE HANDCUFFS PROVIDED BY CAPTAIN FIELDS OF THE CAMBRIDGE POLICE--
AND HAVE FOUND THEM TO BE UP TO REGULATION STANDARDS!
CH
WE WILL NOW PROCEED TO THE HARVARD BRIDGE--
WHERE I WILL PERFORM A FEAT THE LIKES OF WHICH YOU HAVE NEVER SEEN!

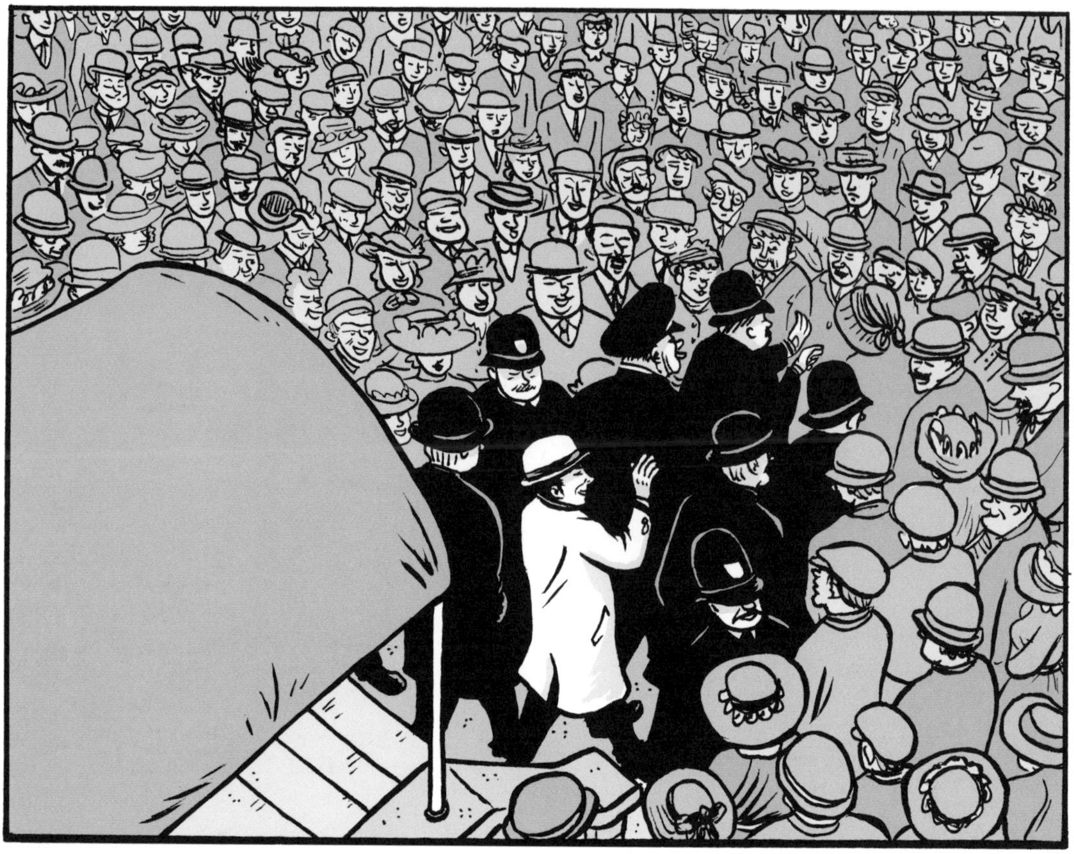

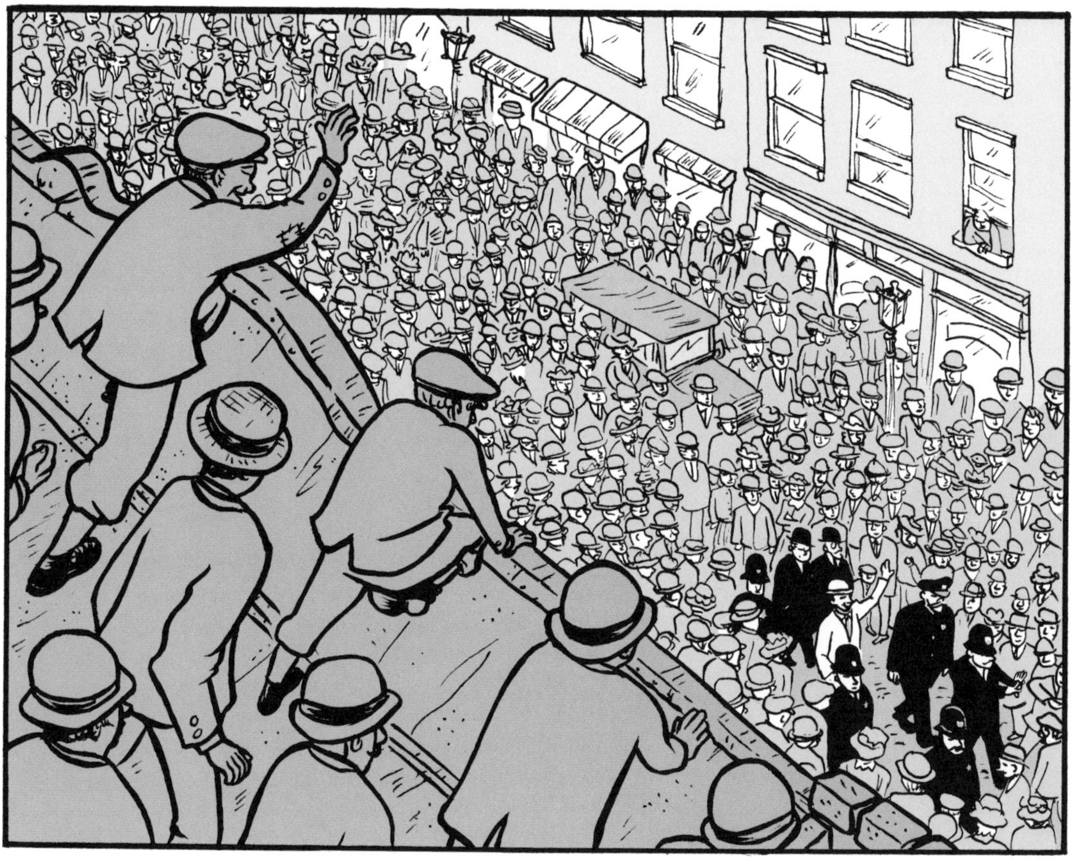

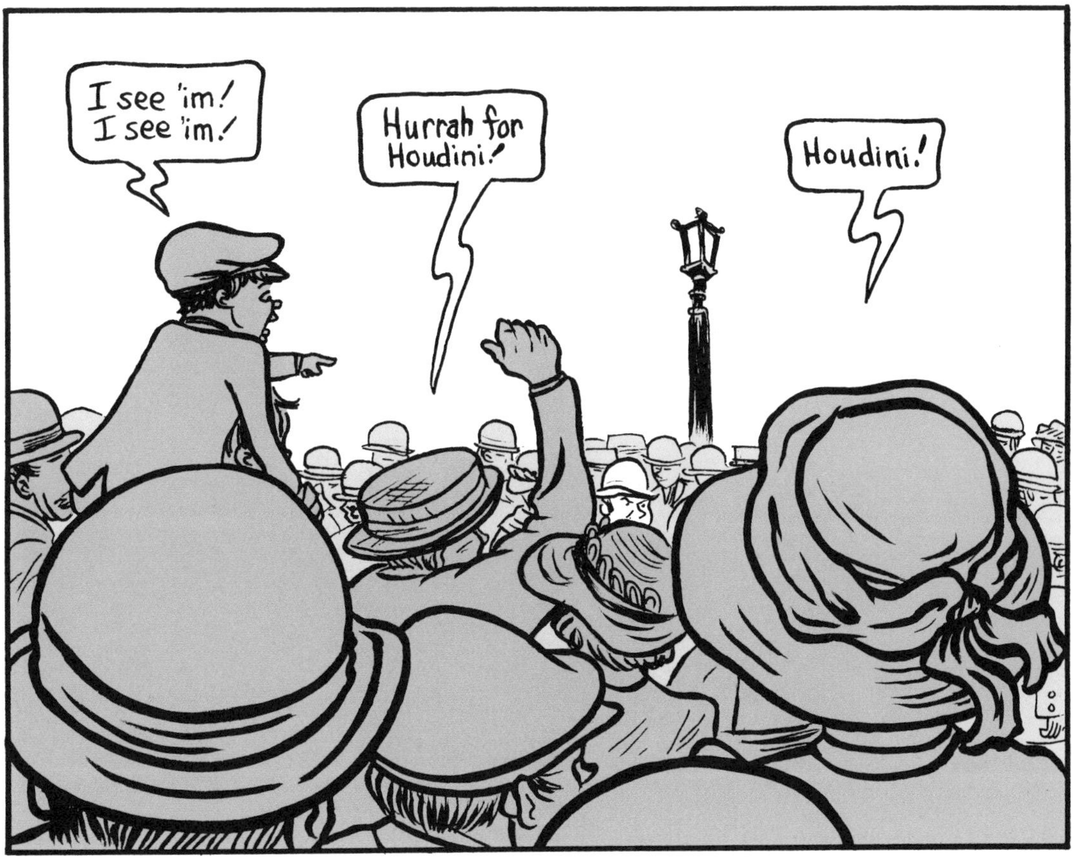
I see 'im!
I see 'im!
Hurrah for Houdini!
Houdini!

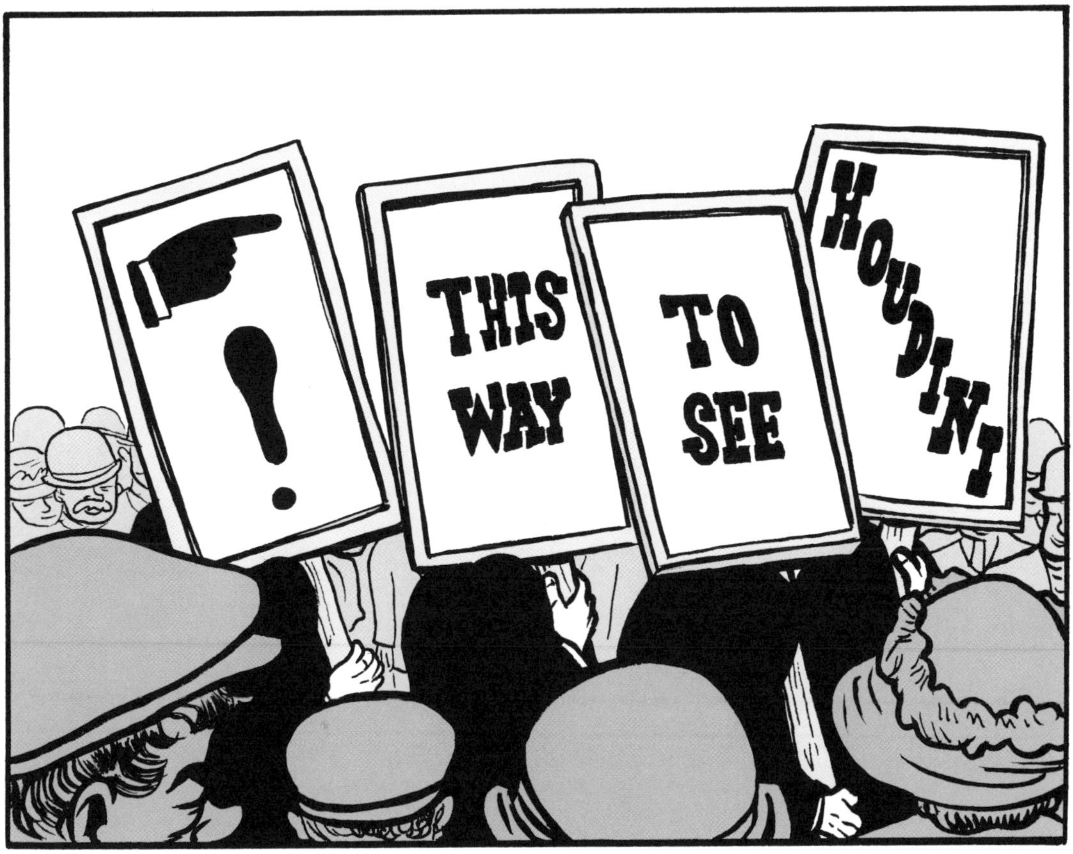
THIS WAY
TO SEE
HOUDINI

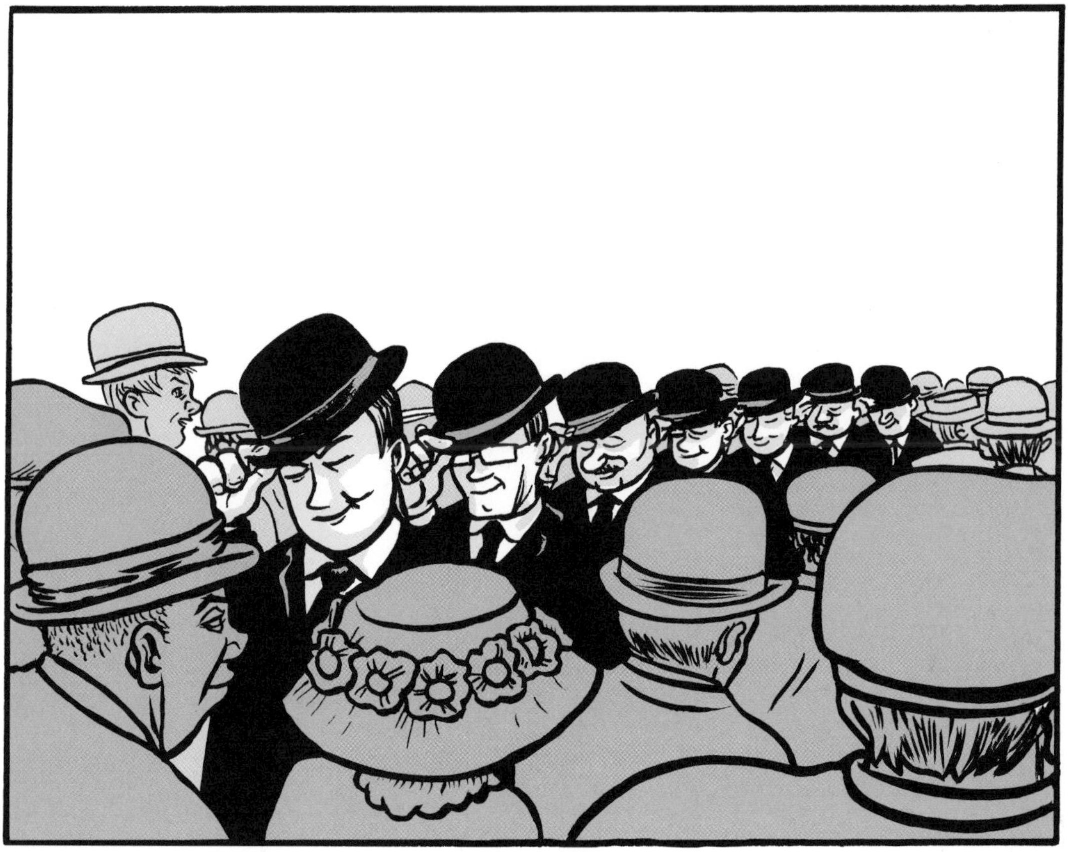

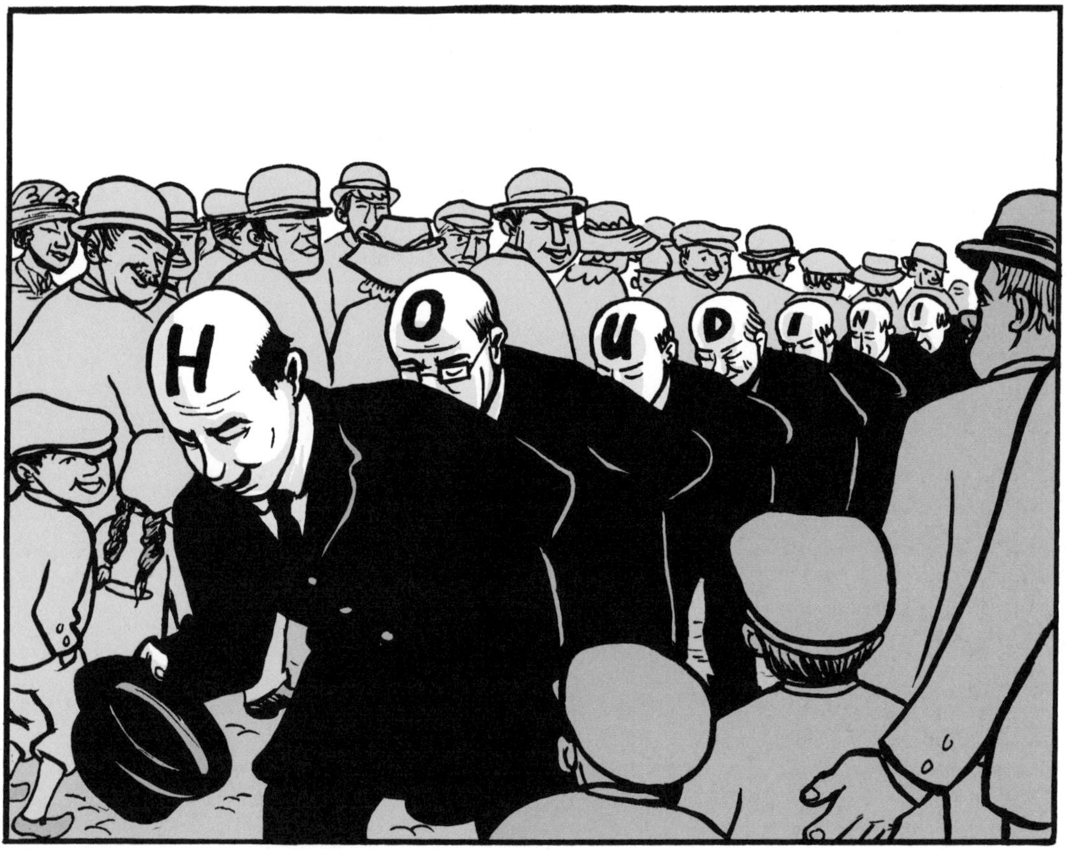
H
O
U
D
N

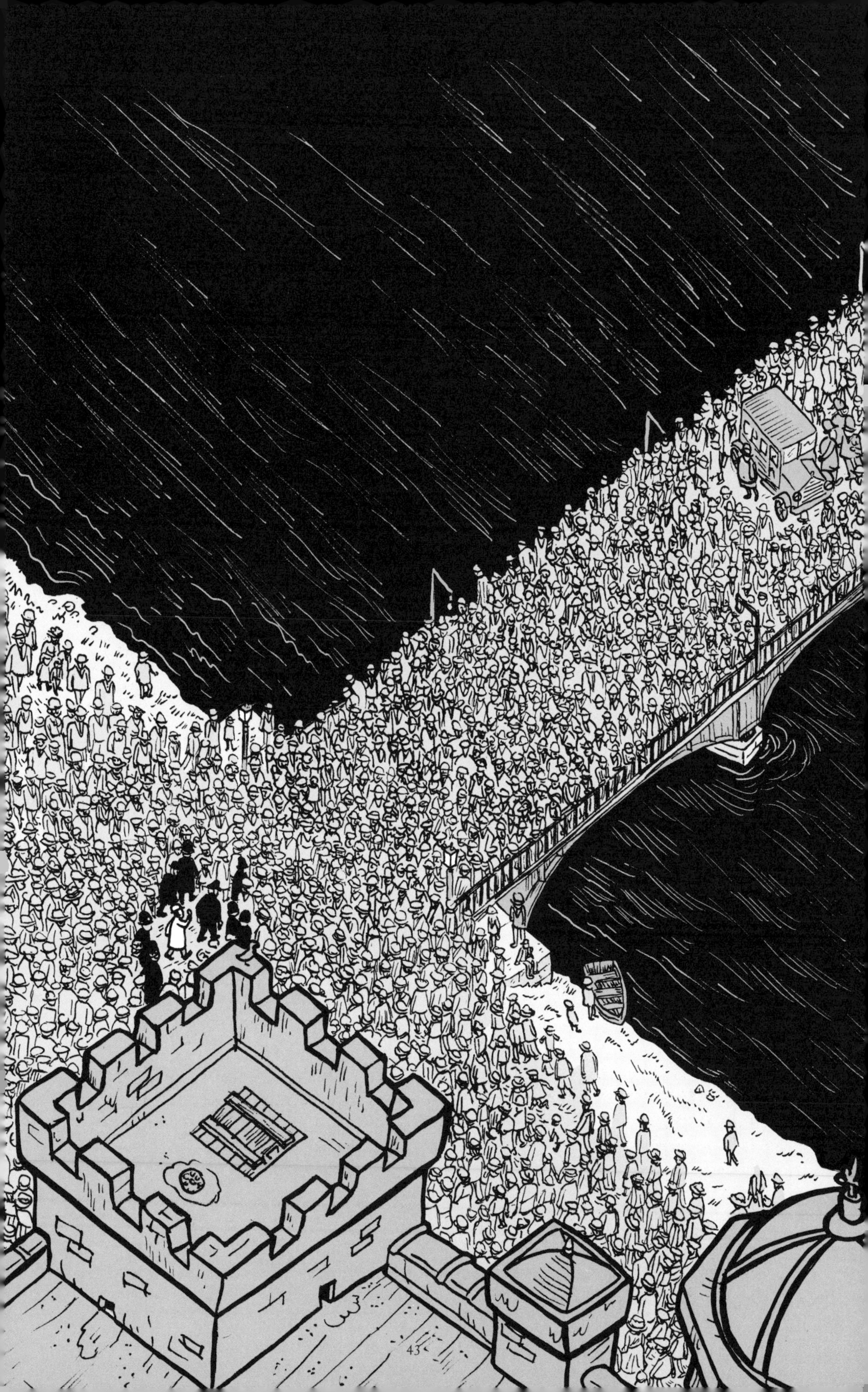

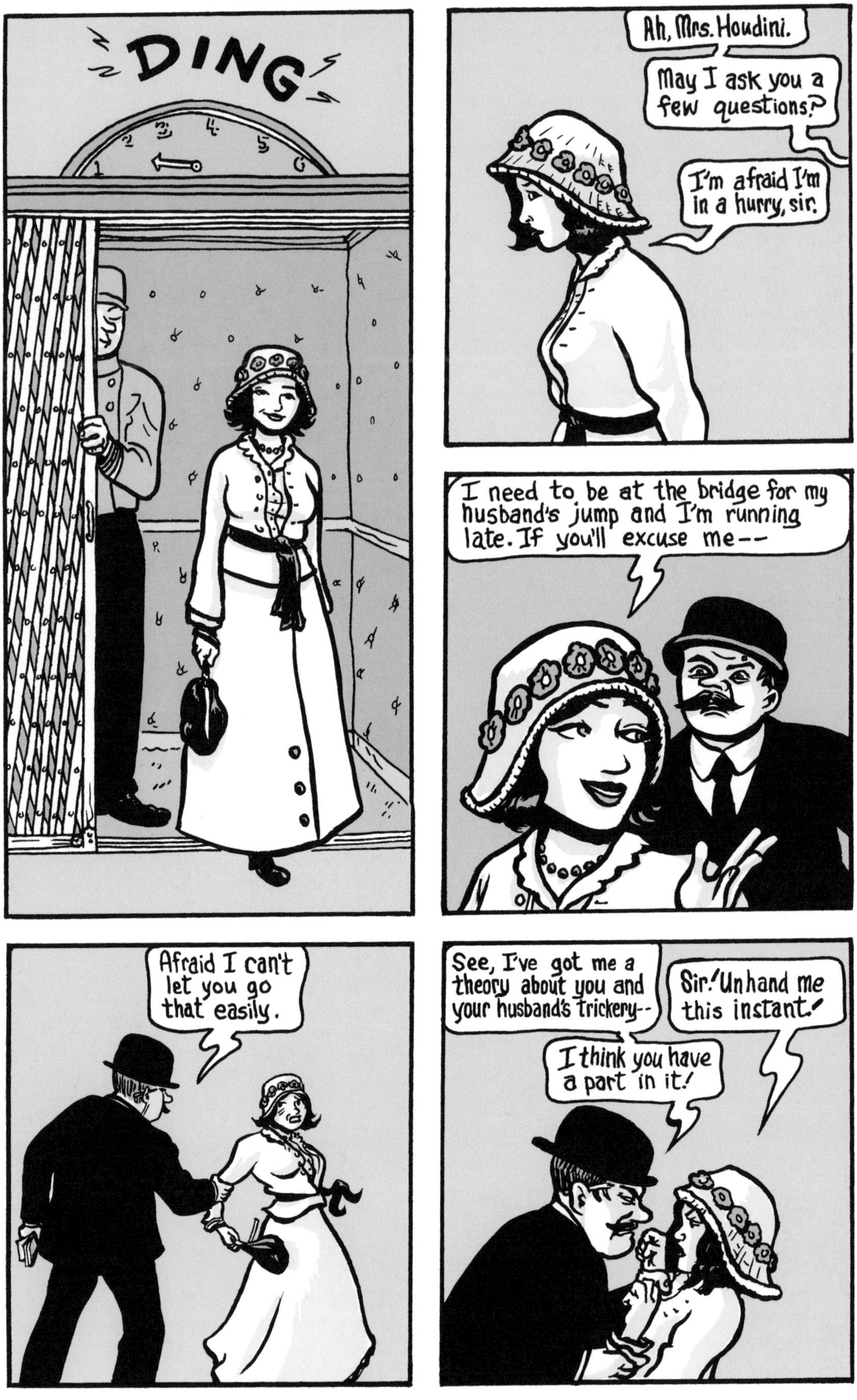
DING
Ah, Mrs. Houdini.
May I ask you a few questions?
I'm afraid I'm in a hurry, sir.
I need to be at the bridge for my husband's jump and I'm running late. If you'll excuse me--
Afraid I can't let you go that easily.
See, I've got me a theory about you and your husband's trickery--
I think you have a part in it!
Sir! Unhand me this instant!

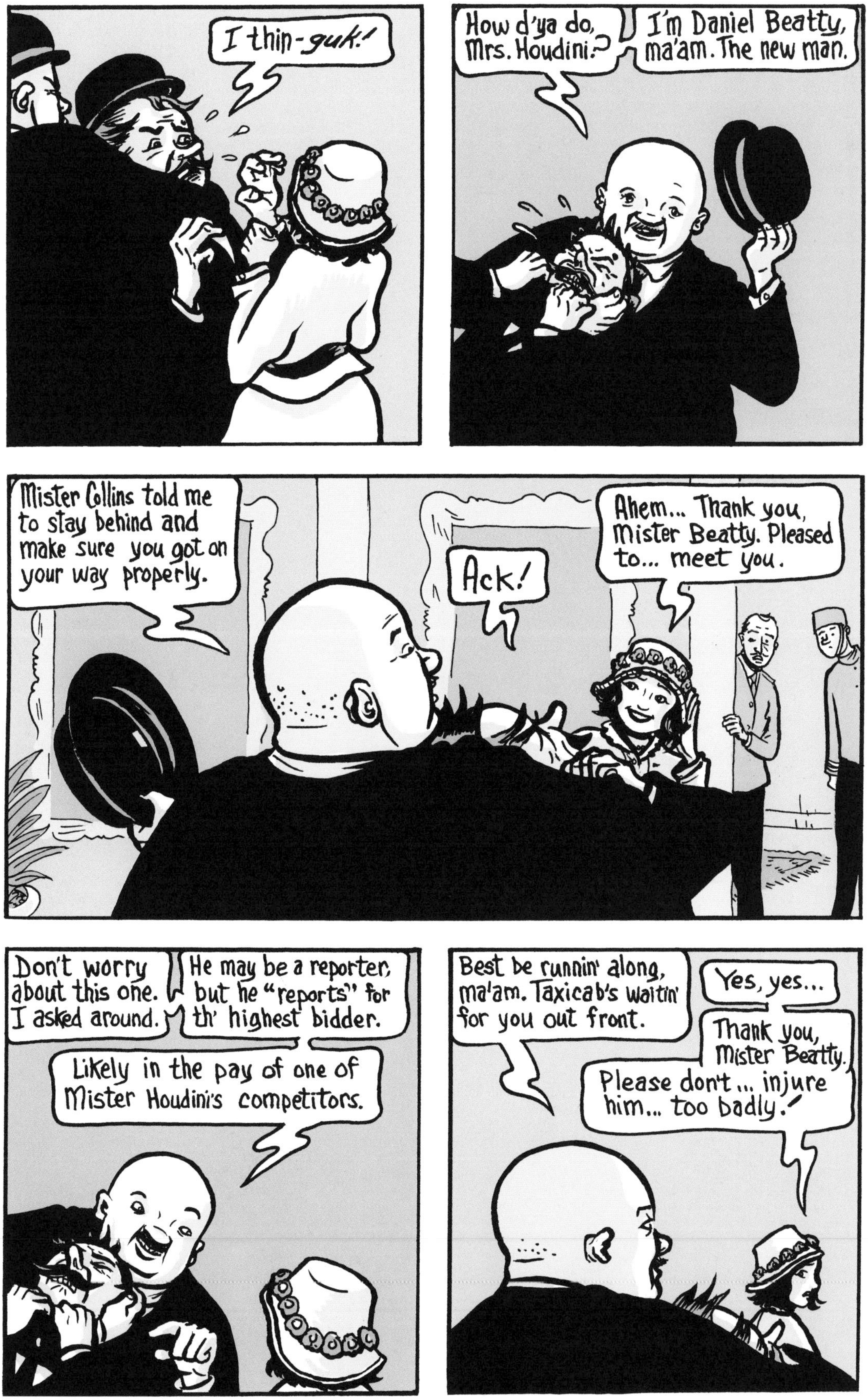
I thin-guk!
How d'ya do, Mrs. Houdini?
I'm Daniel Beatty, ma'am. The new man.
Mister Collins told me to stay behind and make sure you got on your way properly.
Ack!
Ahem... Thank you, Mister Beatty. Pleased to... meet you.
Don't worry about this one. I asked around.
He may be a reporter, but he "reports" for th' highest bidder.
Likely in the pay of one of Mister Houdini's competitors.
Best be runnin' along, ma'am. Taxicab's waitin' for you out front.
Yes, yes...
Thank you, Mister Beatty.
Please don't... injure him... too badly.

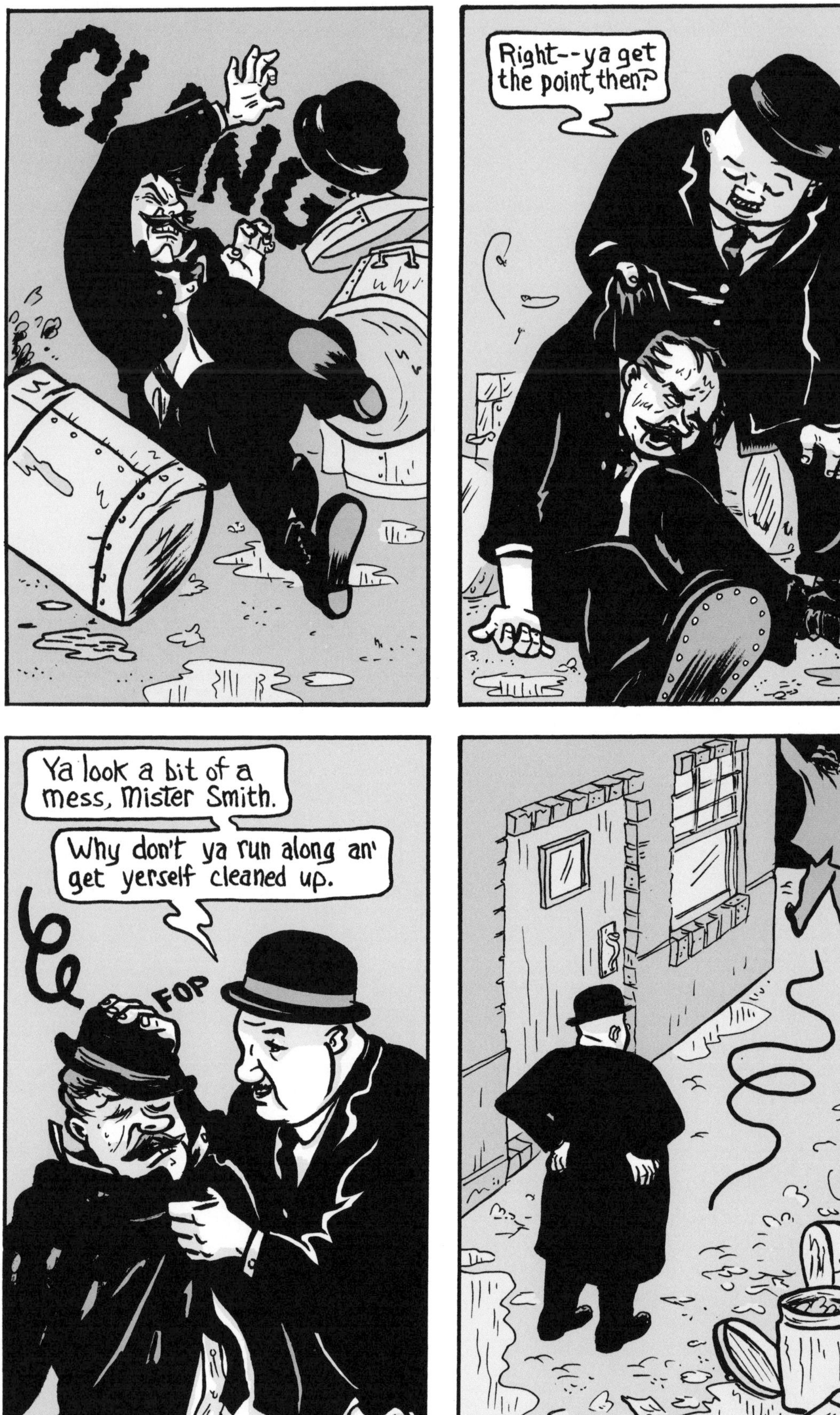
CLANG
Right--ya get the point, then?
Ya look a bit of a mess, Mister Smith.
Why don't ya run along an' get yerself cleaned up.
FOP

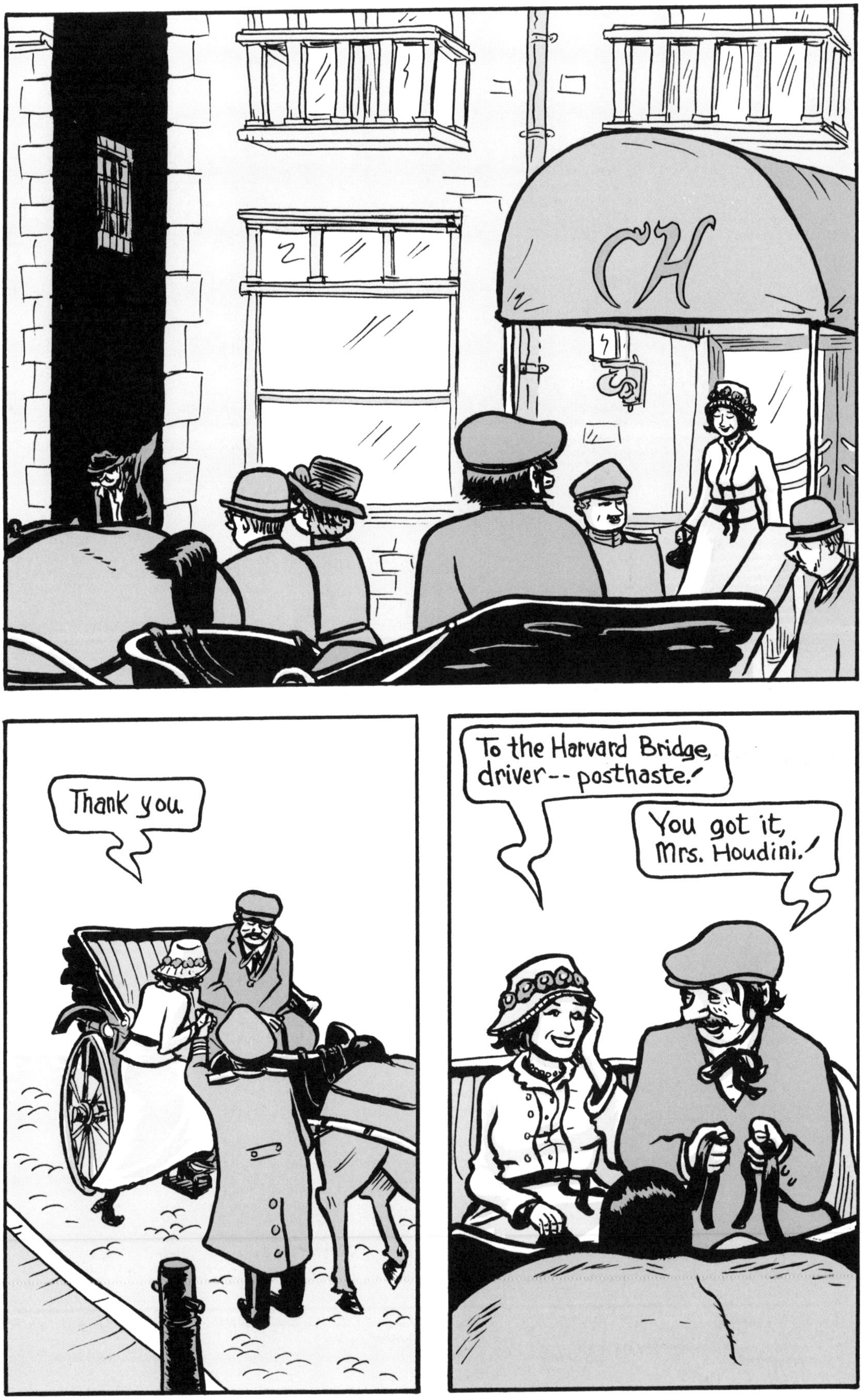

Thank you.
To the Harvard Bridge, driver-- posthaste!
You got it, Mrs. Houdini!

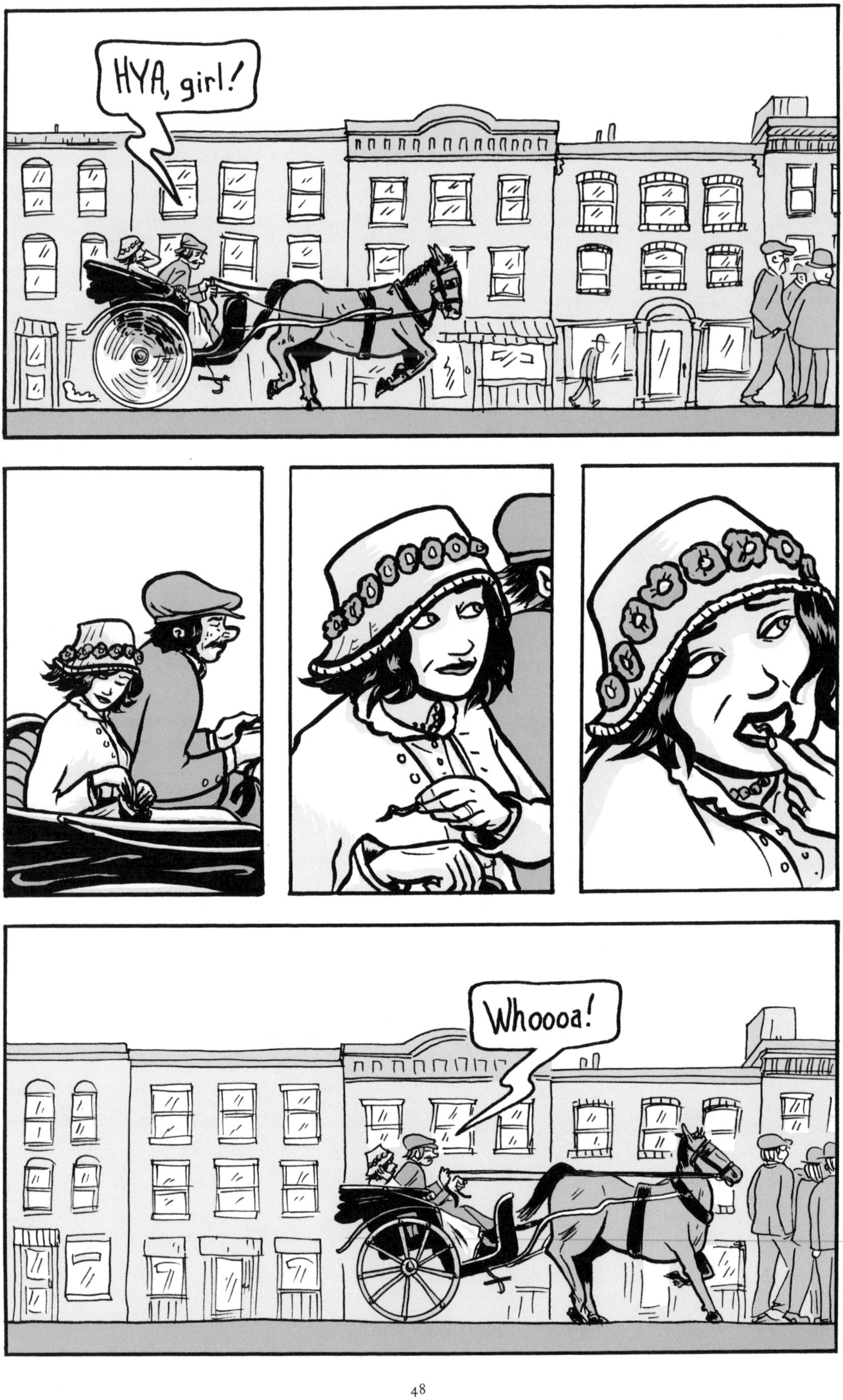
HYA, girl!
Whoooa!

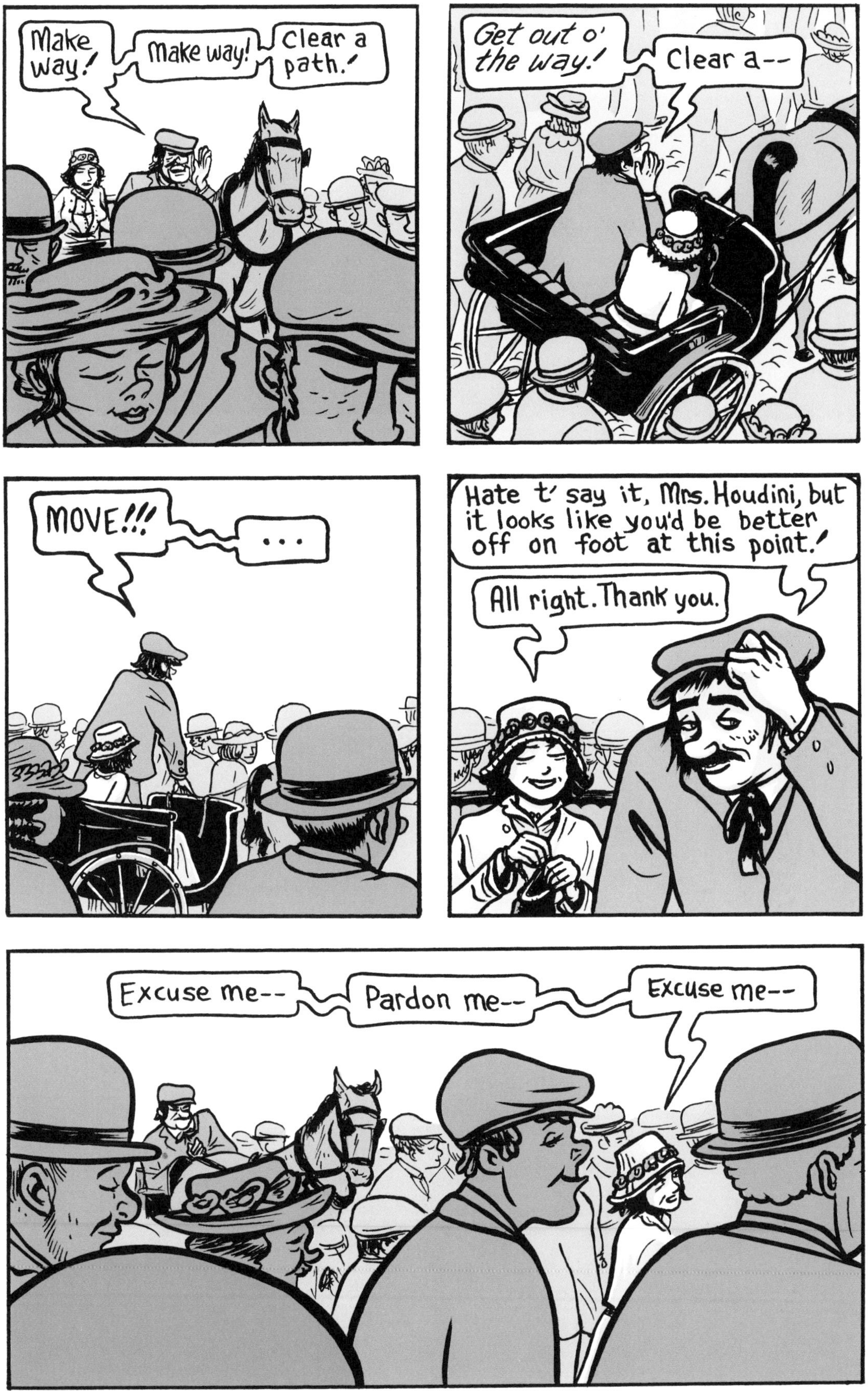
Make way!
Make way!
Clear a path.
Get out o' the way!
Clear a--
MOVE!!!
...
Hate t' say it, Mrs. Houdini, but it looks like you'd be better off on foot at this point.
All right. Thank you.
Excuse me--
Pardon me--
Excuse me--

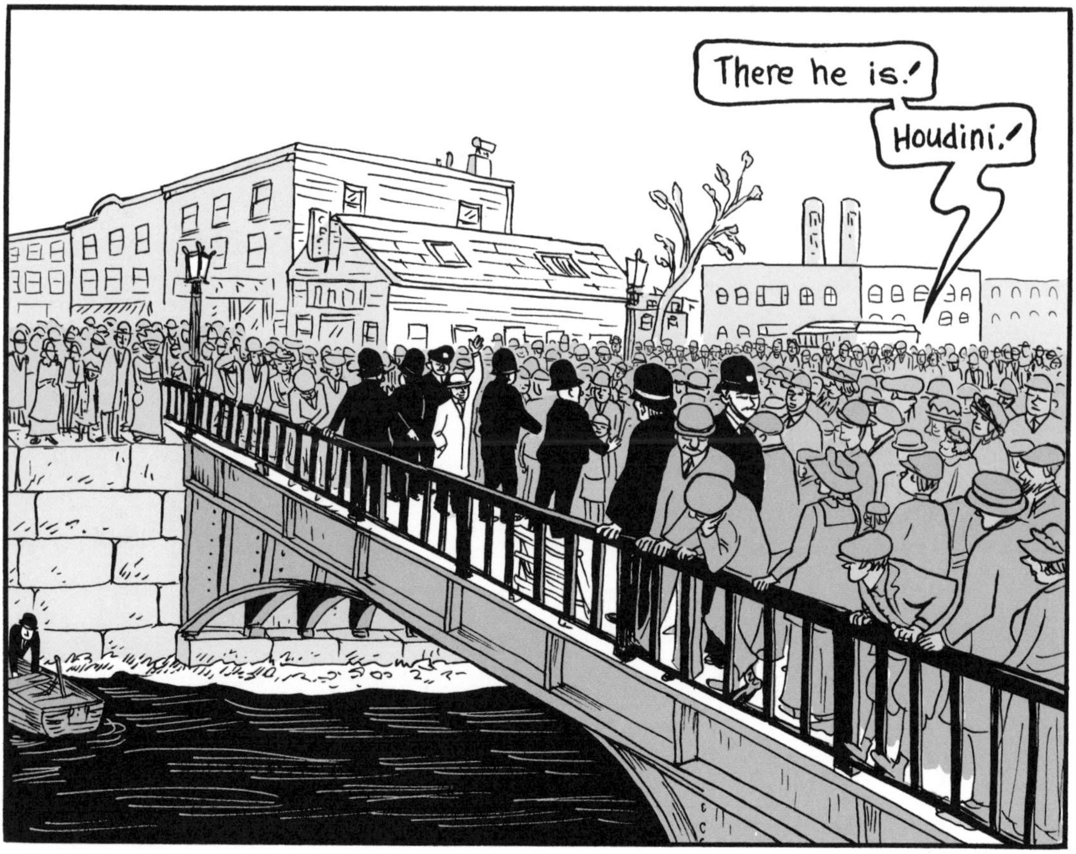
There he is!
Houdini!

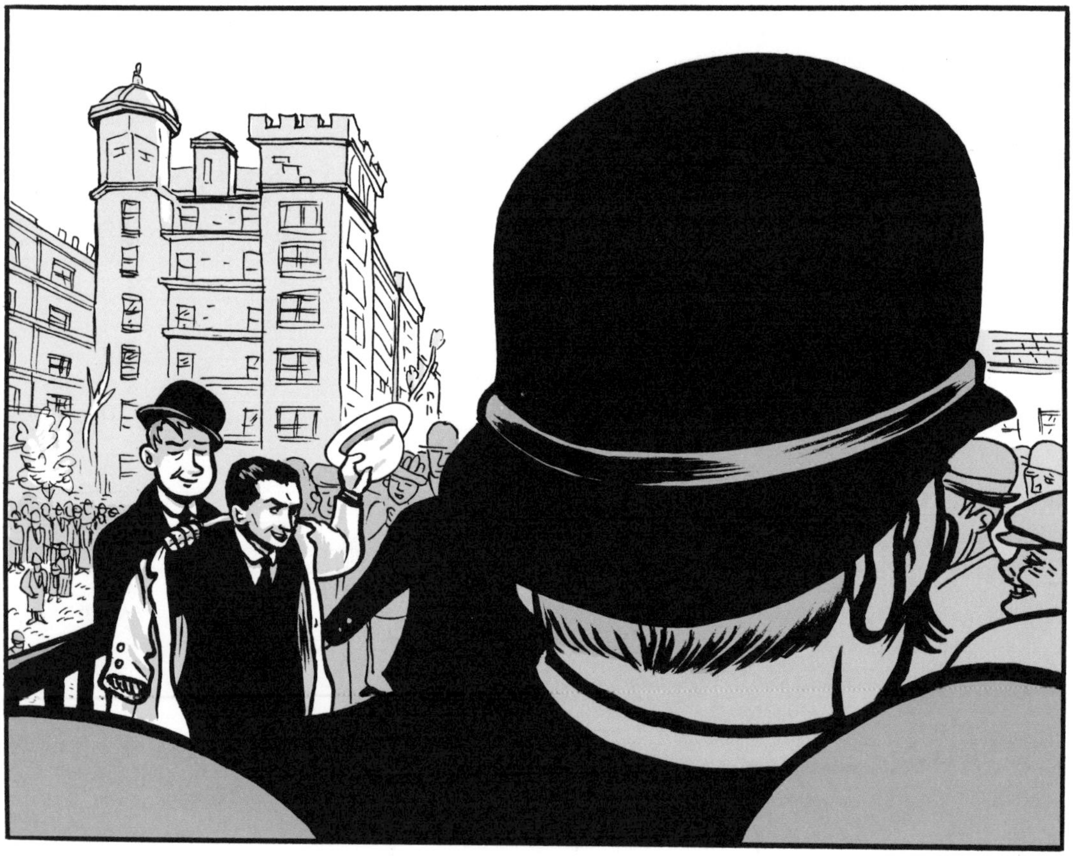

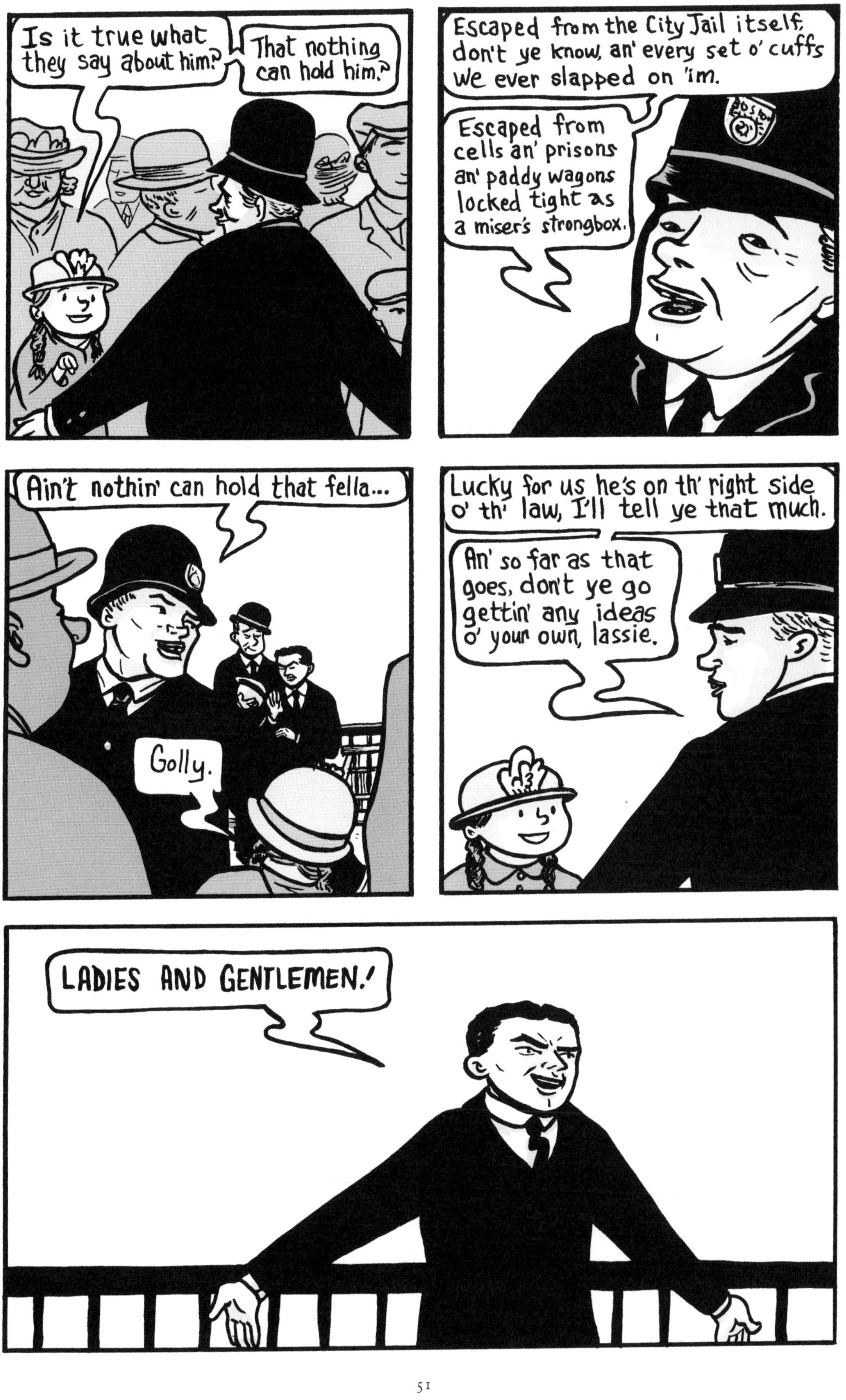
Is it true what they say about him?
That nothing can hold him?
Escaped from the City Jail itself, don't ye know, an' every set o' cuffs we ever slapped on 'im.
Escaped from cells an' prisons an' paddy wagons locked tight as a miser's strongbox.
Ain't nothin' can hold that fella...
Golly.
Lucky for us he's on th' right side o' th' law, I'll tell ye that much.
An' so far as that goes, don't ye go gettin' any ideas o' your own, lassie.
LADIES AND GENTLEMEN!

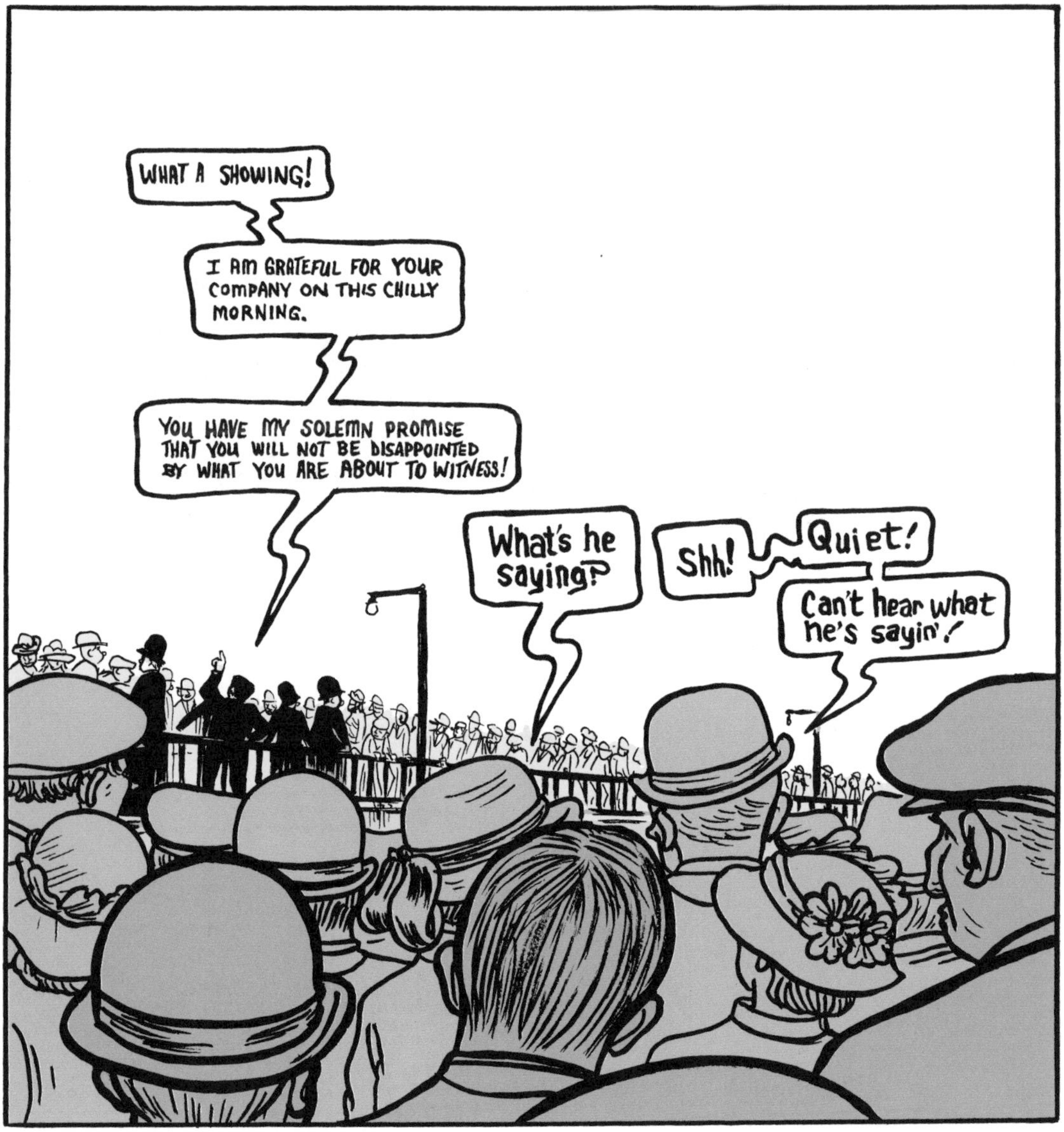
WHAT A SHOWING!
I AM GRATEFUL FOR YOUR COMPANY ON THIS CHILLY MORNING.
YOU HAVE MY SOLEMN PROMISE THAT YOU WILL NOT BE DISAPPOINTED BY WHAT YOU ARE ABOUT TO WITNESS!
What's he saying?
Shh!
Quiet!
Can't hear what he's sayin'!

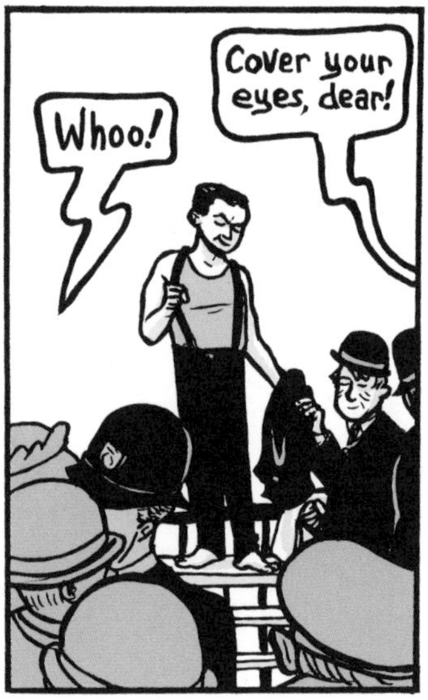
Whoo!
Cover your eyes, dear!

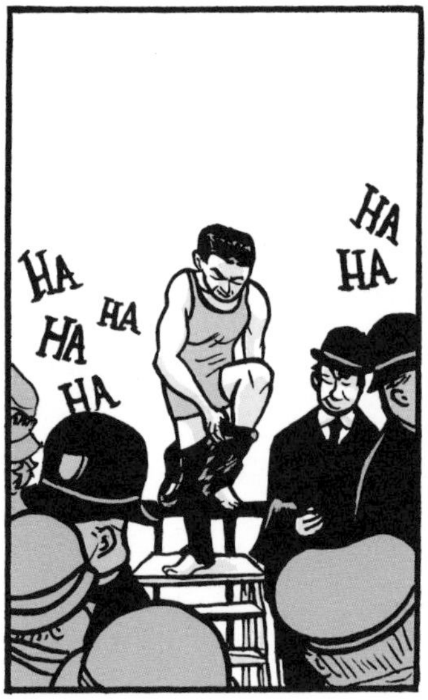
HA
HA
HA
HA
HA
HA

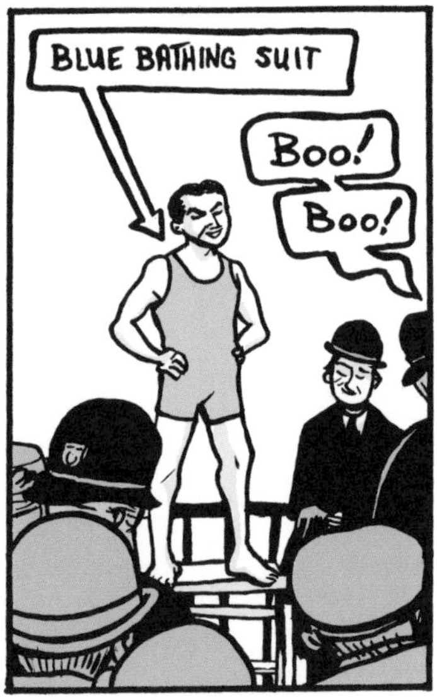
BLUE BATHING SUIT
Boo!
Boo!

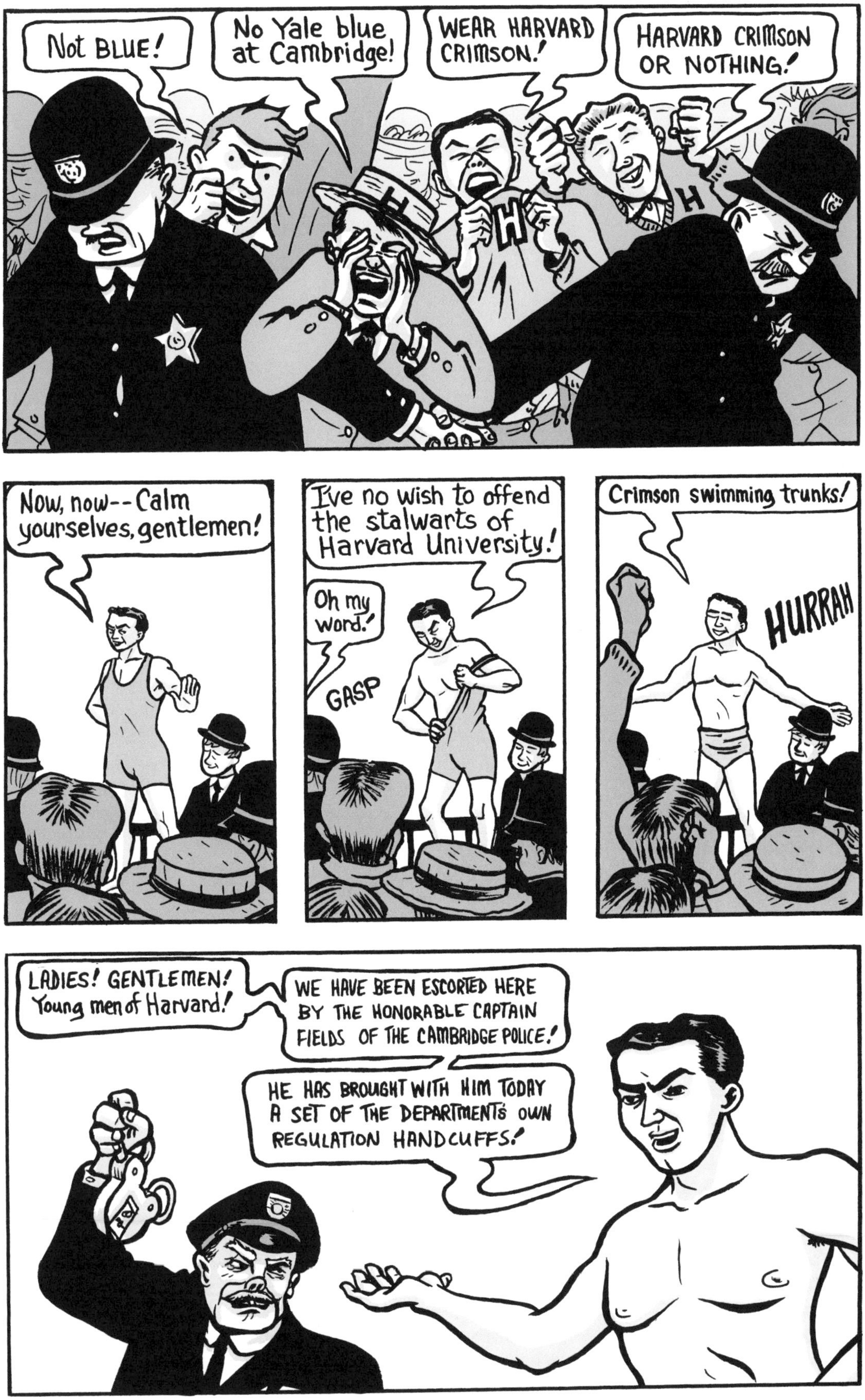
Not BLUE!
No Yale blue at Cambridge!
WEAR HARVARD CRIMSON!
HARVARD CRIMSON OR NOTHING!
Now, now--Calm yourselves, gentlemen!
I've no wish to offend the stalwarts of Harvard University!
Oh my word!
GASP
Crimson swimming trunks!
HURRAH
LADIES! GENTLEMEN! Young men of Harvard!
WE HAVE BEEN ESCORTED HERE BY THE HONORABLE CAPTAIN FIELDS OF THE CAMBRIDGE POLICE!
HE HAS BROUGHT WITH HIM TODAY A SET OF THE DEPARTMENT'S OWN REGULATION HANDCUFFS!

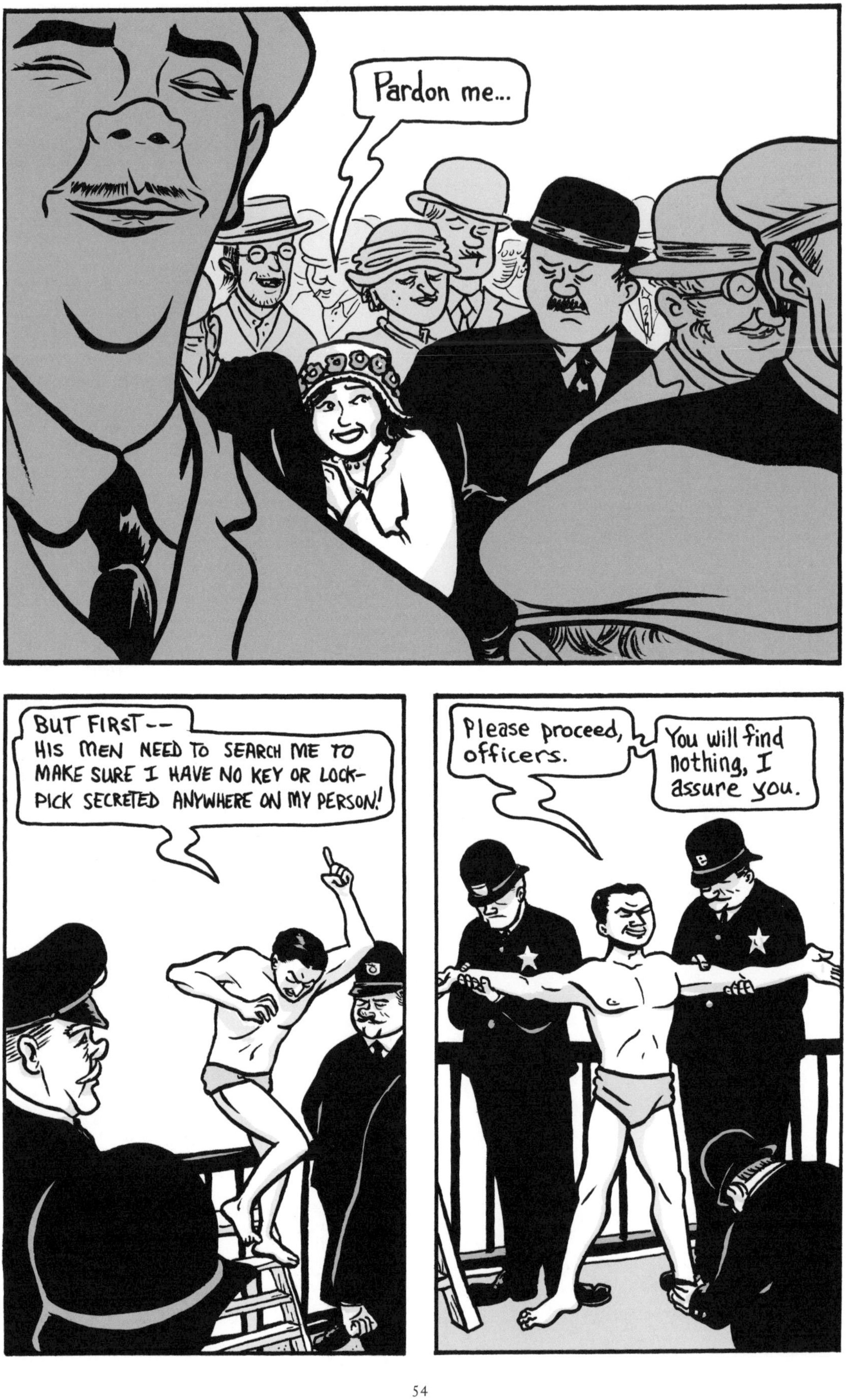
Pardon me...
BUT FIRST-- HIS MEN NEED TO SEARCH ME TO MAKE SURE I HAVE NO KEY OR LOCK-PICK SECRETED ANYWHERE ON MY PERSON!
Please proceed, officers.
You will find nothing, I assure you.

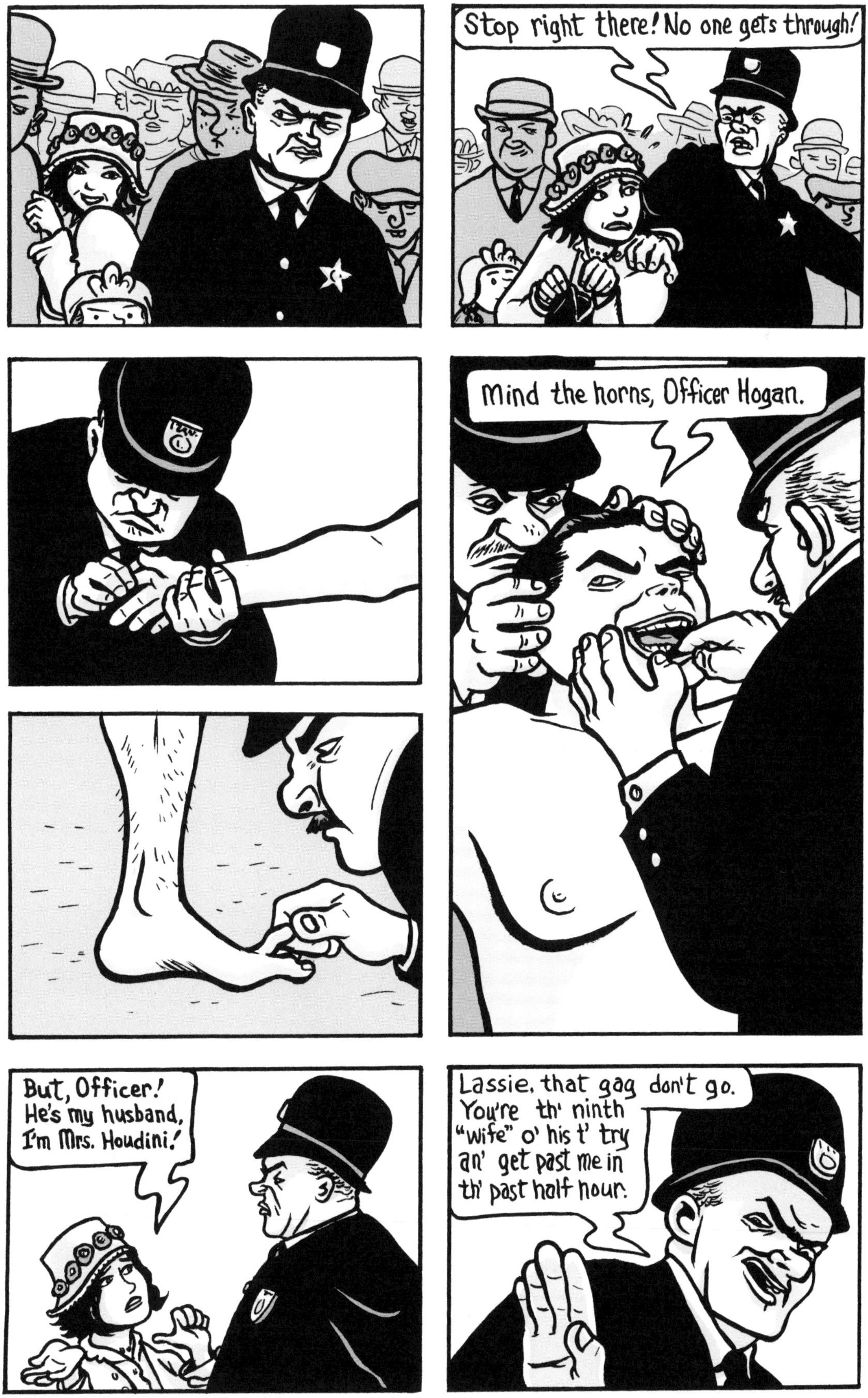
Stop right there! No one gets through!
Mind the horns, Officer Hogan.
But, Officer! He's my husband, I'm Mrs. Houdini!
Lassie, that gag don't go. You're th' ninth "wife" o' his t' try an' get past me in th' past half hour.

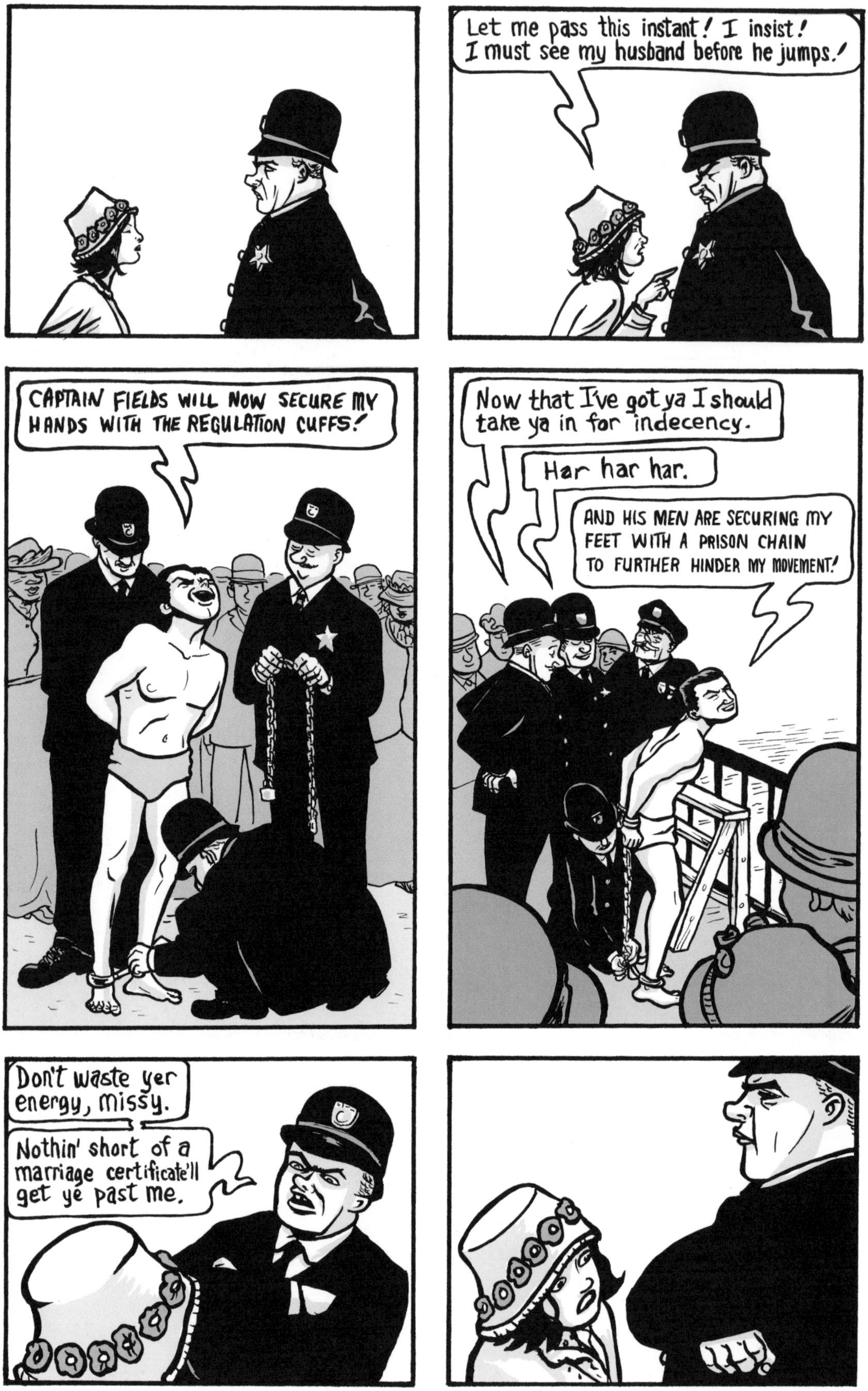
Let me pass this instant! I insist! I must see my husband before he jumps.!
CAPTAIN FIELDS WILL NOW SECURE MY HANDS WITH THE REGULATION CUFFS!
Now that I've got ya I should take ya in for indecency.
Har har har.
AND HIS MEN ARE SECURING MY FEET WITH A PRISON CHAIN TO FURTHER HINDER MY MOVEMENT!
Don't waste yer energy, missy.
Nothin' short of a marriage certificate'll get ye past me.

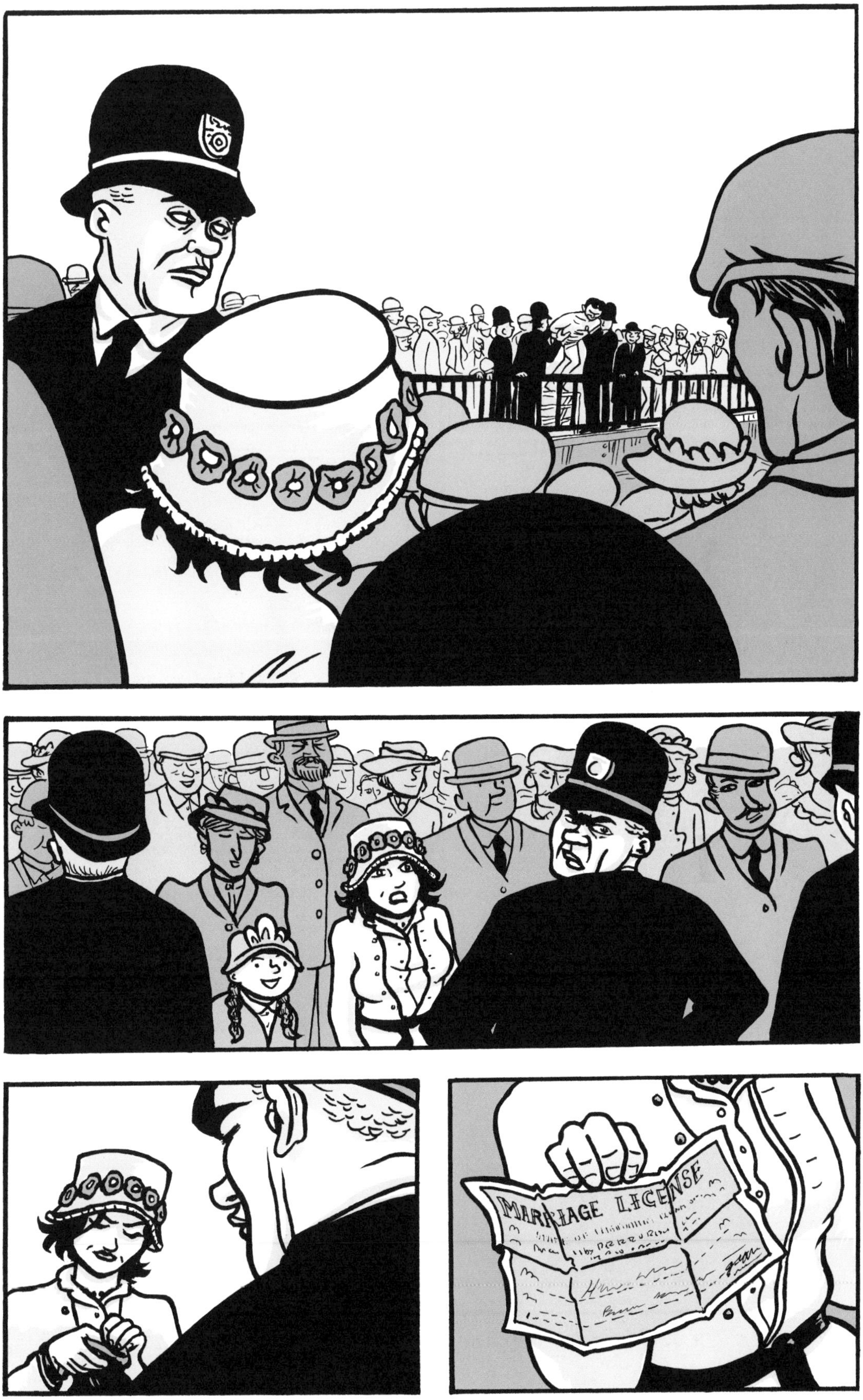
MARRIAGE LICENSE

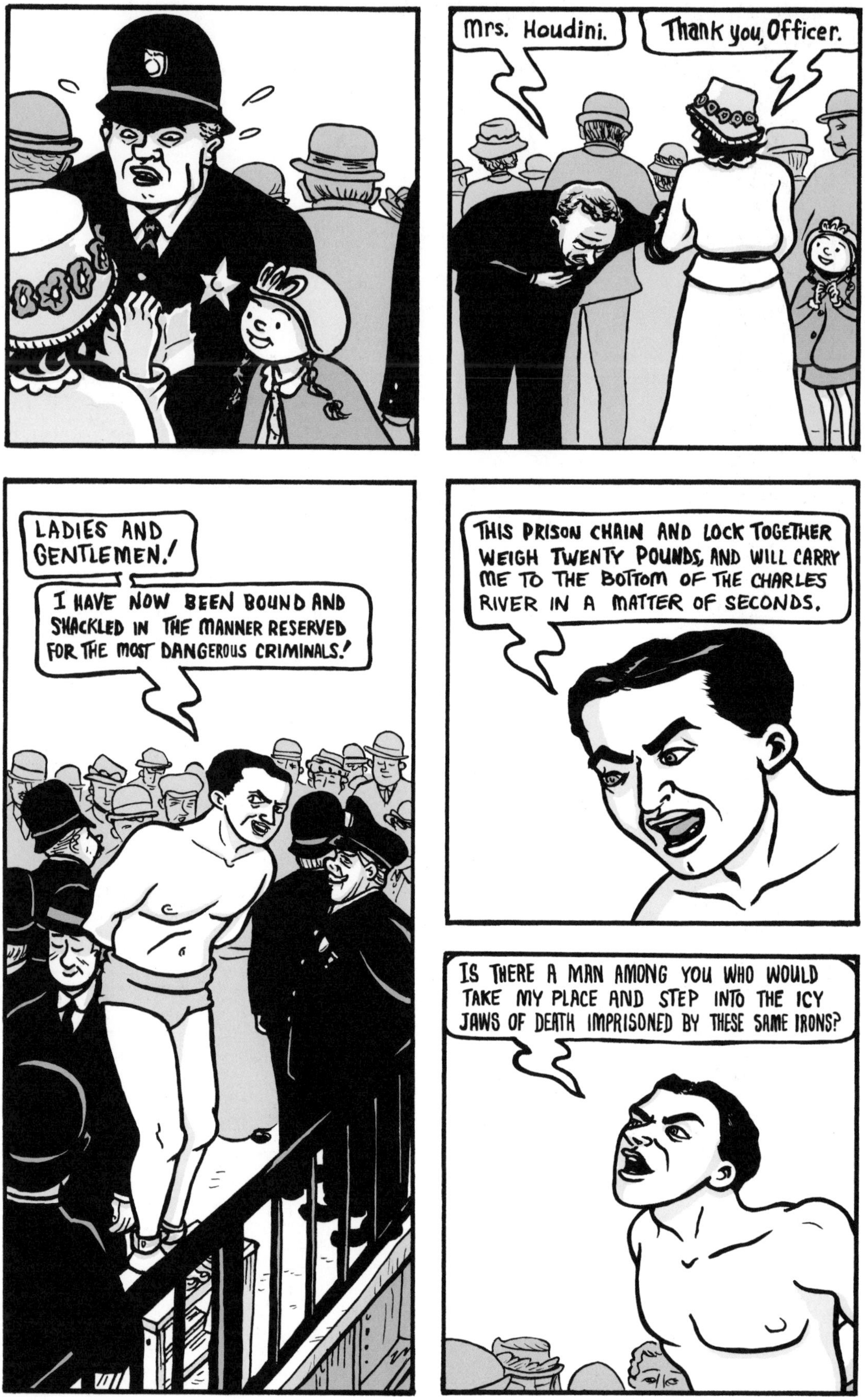
Mrs. Houdini.
Thank you, Officer.
LADIES AND GENTLEMEN!
I HAVE NOW BEEN BOUND AND SHACKLED IN THE MANNER RESERVED FOR THE MOST DANGEROUS CRIMINALS!
THIS PRISON CHAIN AND LOCK TOGETHER WEIGH TWENTY POUNDS, AND WILL CARRY ME TO THE BOTTOM OF THE CHARLES RIVER IN A MATTER OF SECONDS.
IS THERE A MAN AMONG YOU WHO WOULD TAKE MY PLACE AND STEP INTO THE ICY JAWS OF DEATH IMPRISONED BY THESE SAME IRONS?

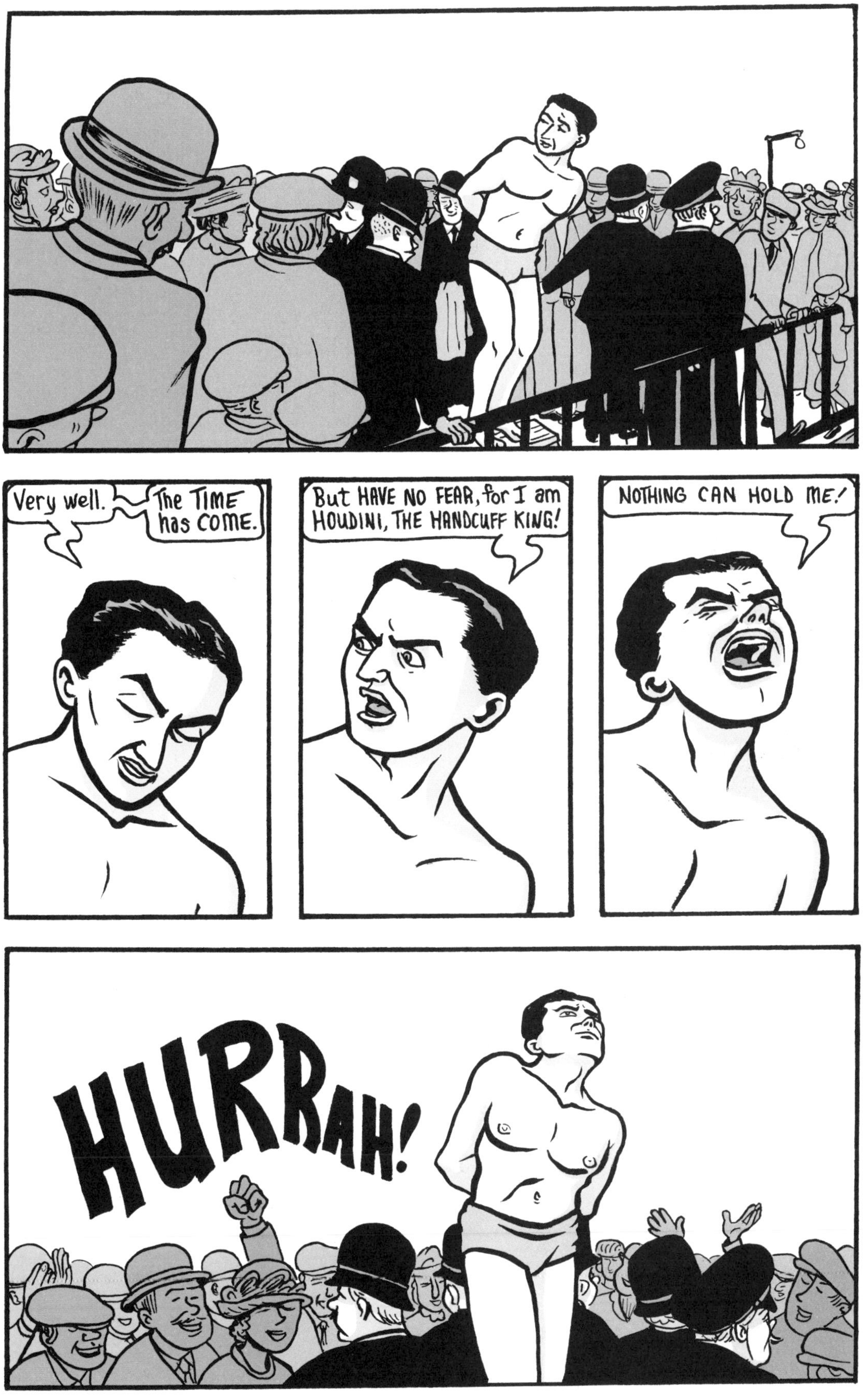
Very well.
The TIME has COME.
But HAVE NO FEAR, for I am HOUDINI, THE HANDCUFF KING!
NOTHING CAN HOLD ME!
HURRAH!

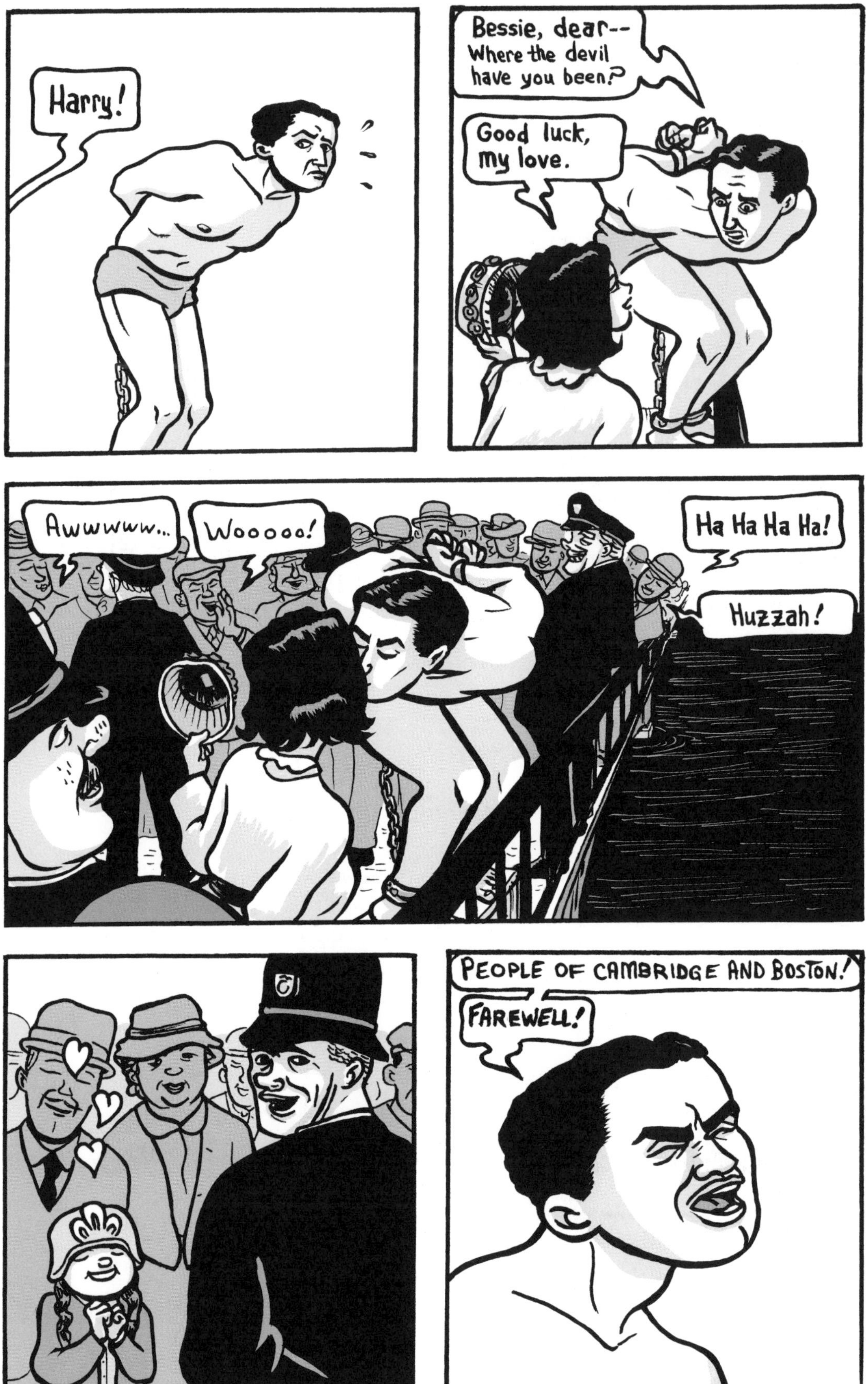
Harry!
Bessie, dear-- Where the devil have you been?
Good luck, my love.
Awwwww...
Wooooo!
Ha Ha Ha Ha!
Huzzah!
PEOPLE OF CAMBRIDGE AND BOSTON!
FAREWELL!

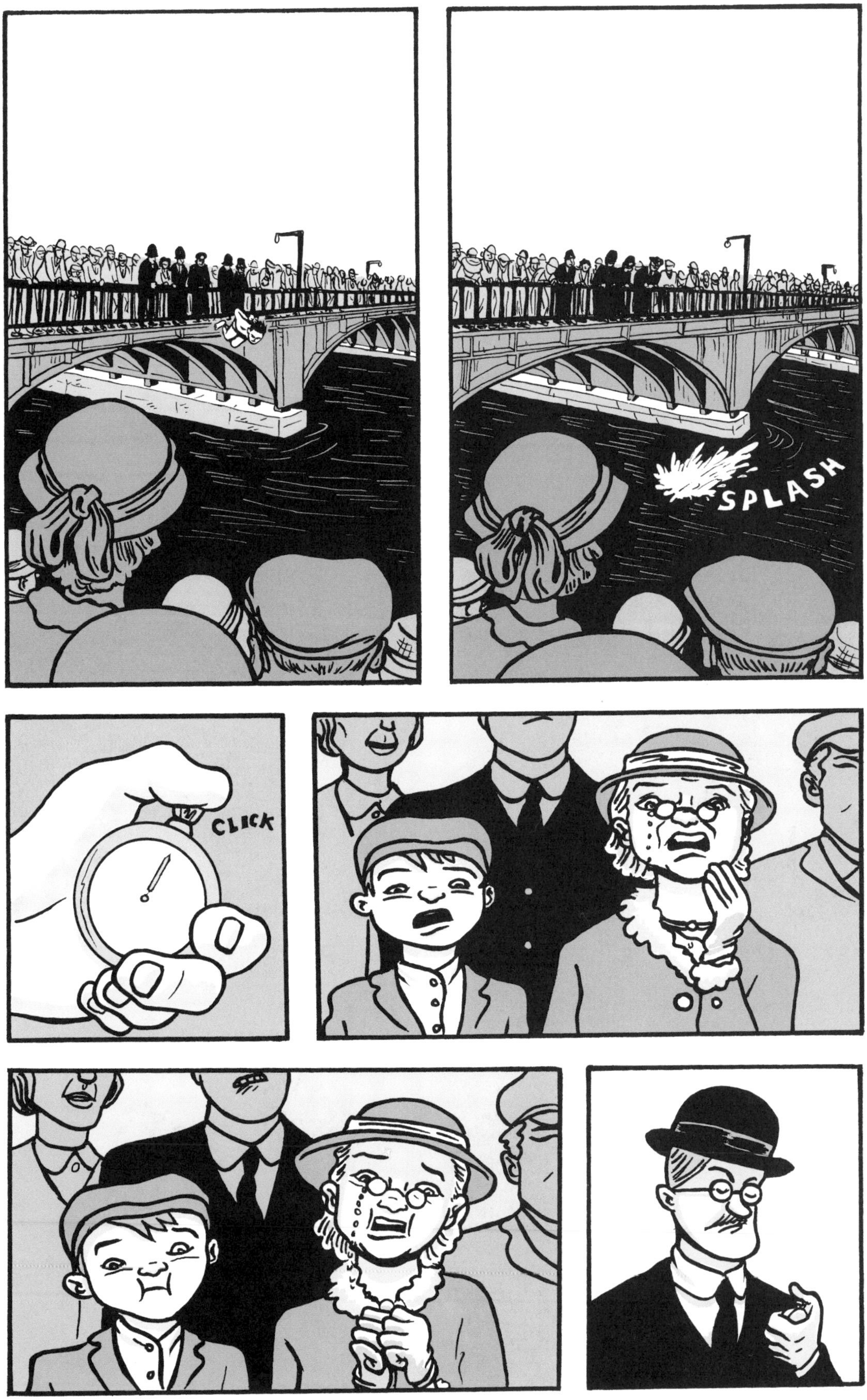
SPLASH
CLICK

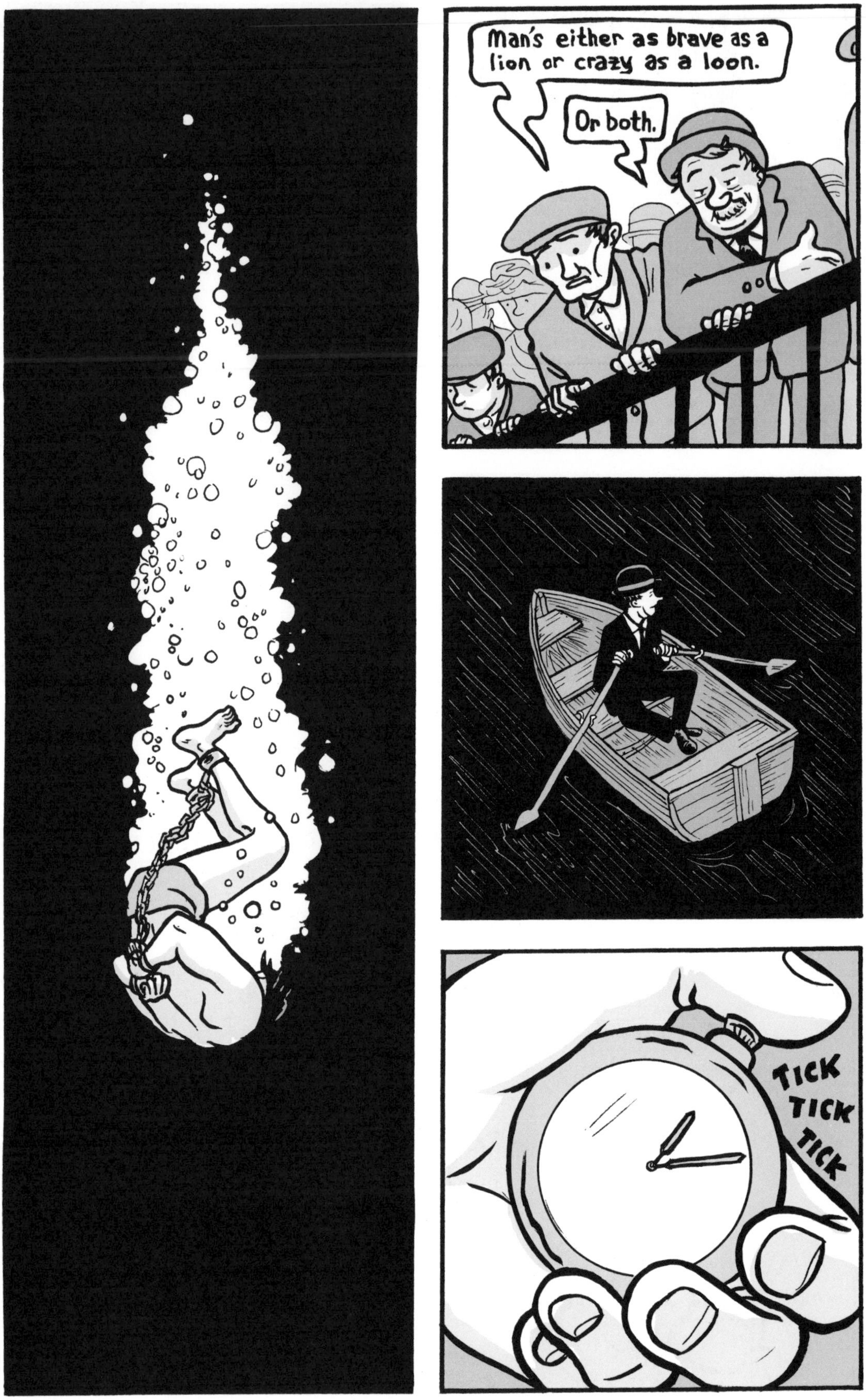
Man's either as brave as a lion or crazy as a loon.
Or both.
TICK
TICK
TICK

Goin' straight to the bottom with all that iron on 'im.

TICK
TICK
TICK

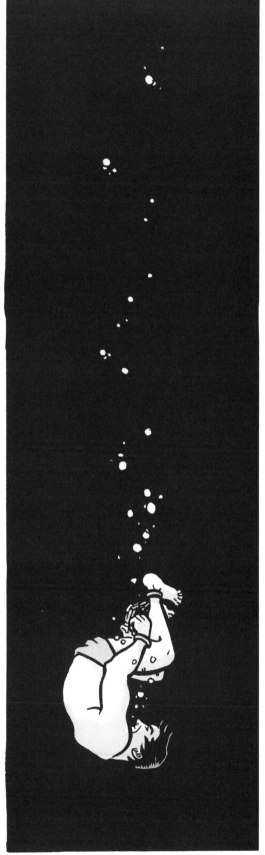

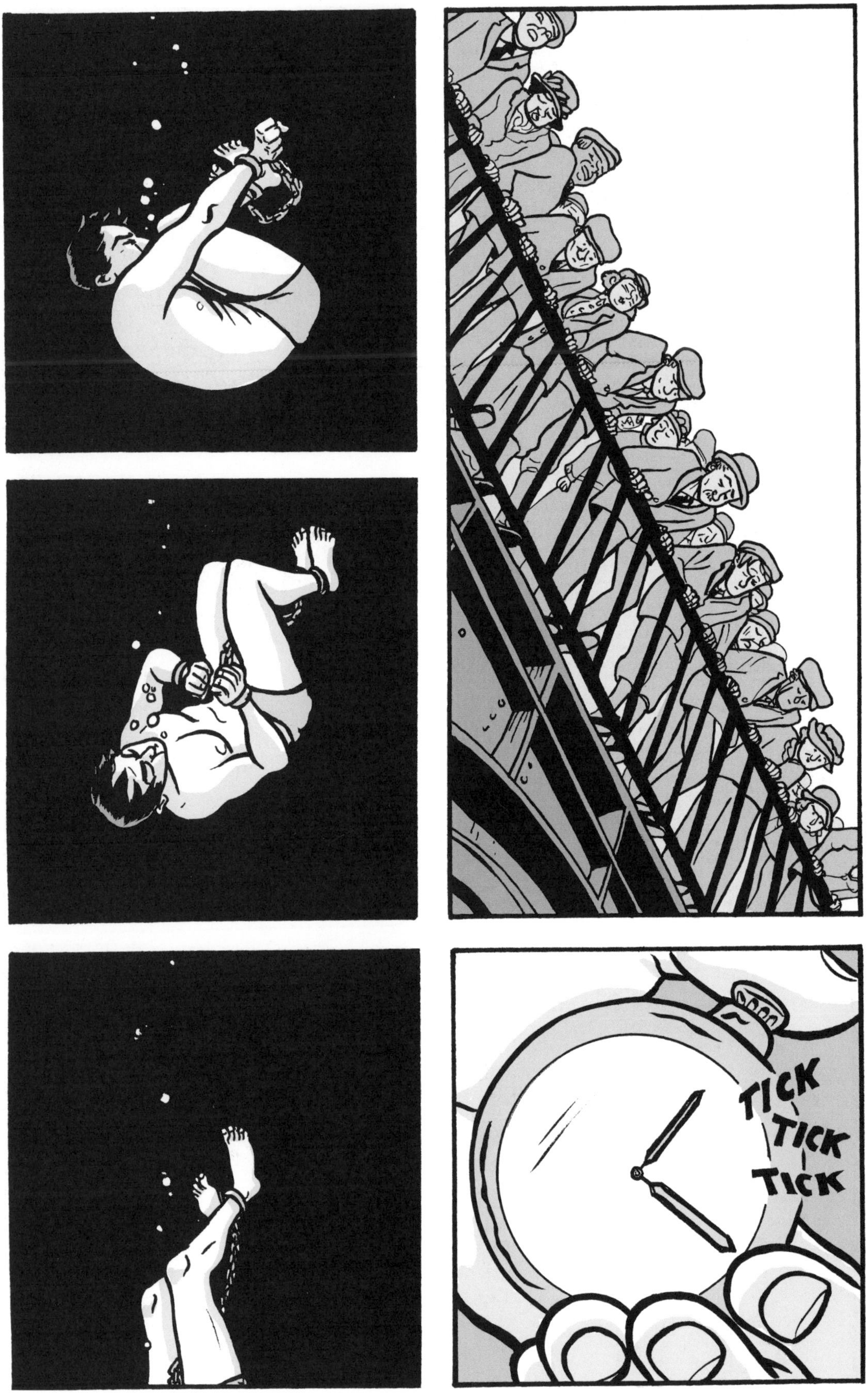
TICK
TICK
TICK

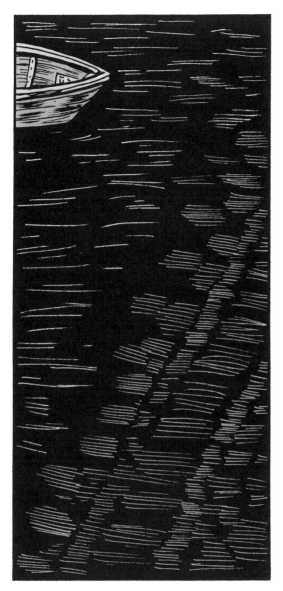

TICK
TICK
TICK

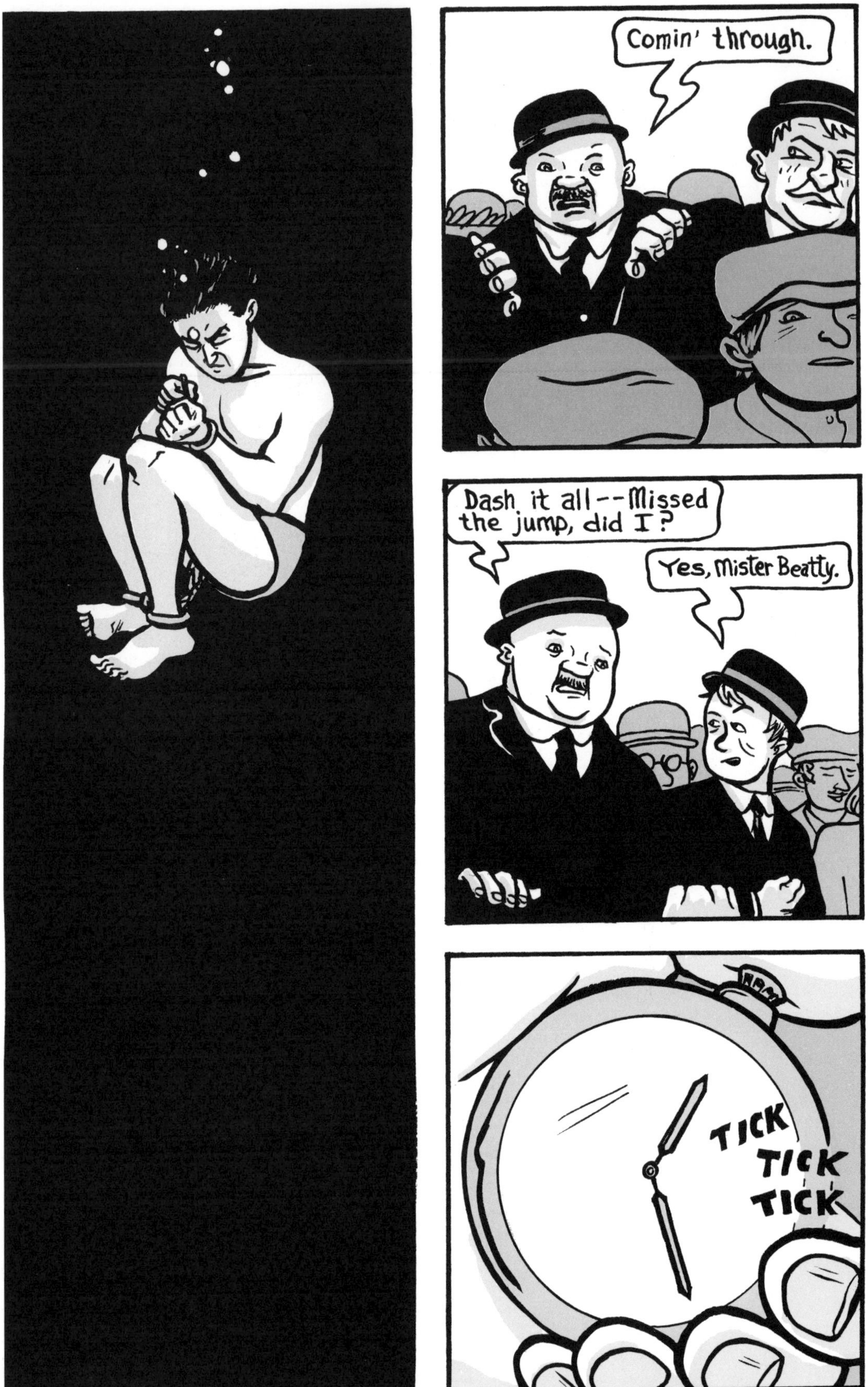
Comin' through.
Dash it all--Missed the jump, did I?
Yes, Mister Beatty.
TICK
TICK
TICK

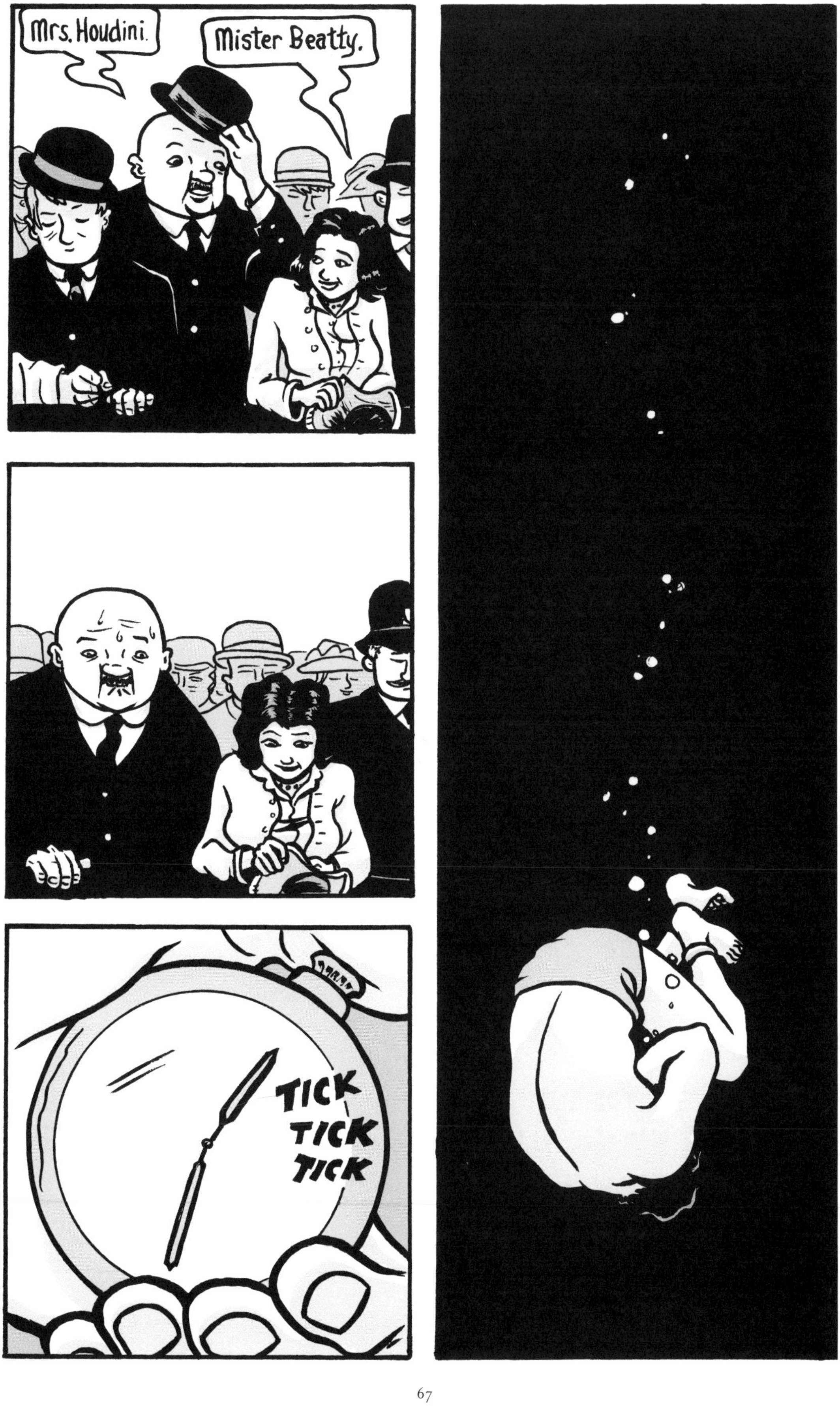
Mrs. Houdini.
Mister Beatty.
TICK
TICK
TICK

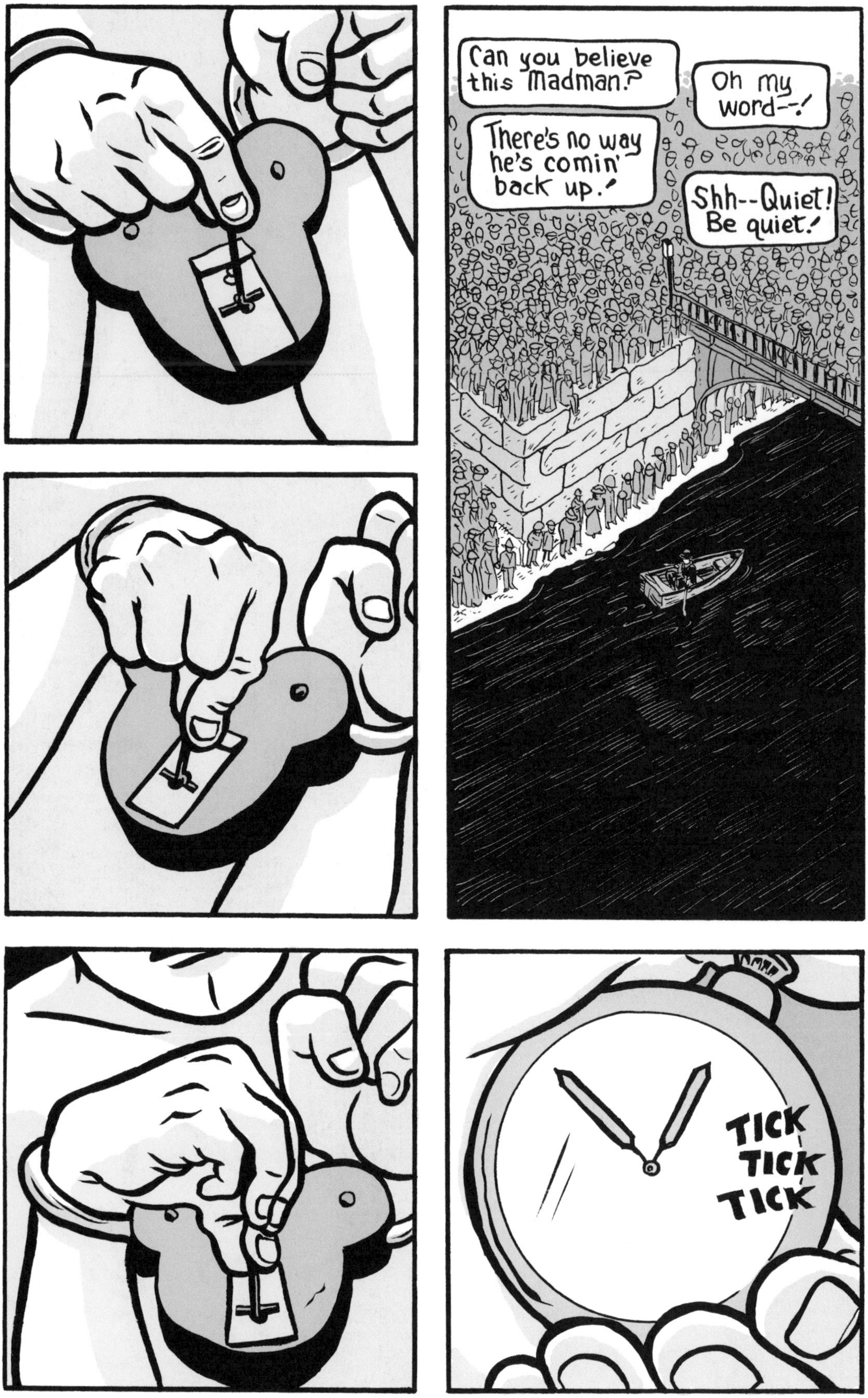

Can you believe this Madman?
Oh my word--!
There's no way he's comin' back up.!
Shh--Quiet! Be quiet!
TICK
TICK
TICK

It's absurd! Risking his life like this!

Nothin' can hold Harry Houdini! Nothin'!

He'll be up in a second, you just watch.

I think I'm going to faint.

TICK TICK TICK

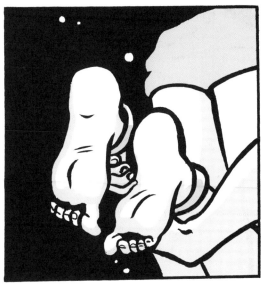

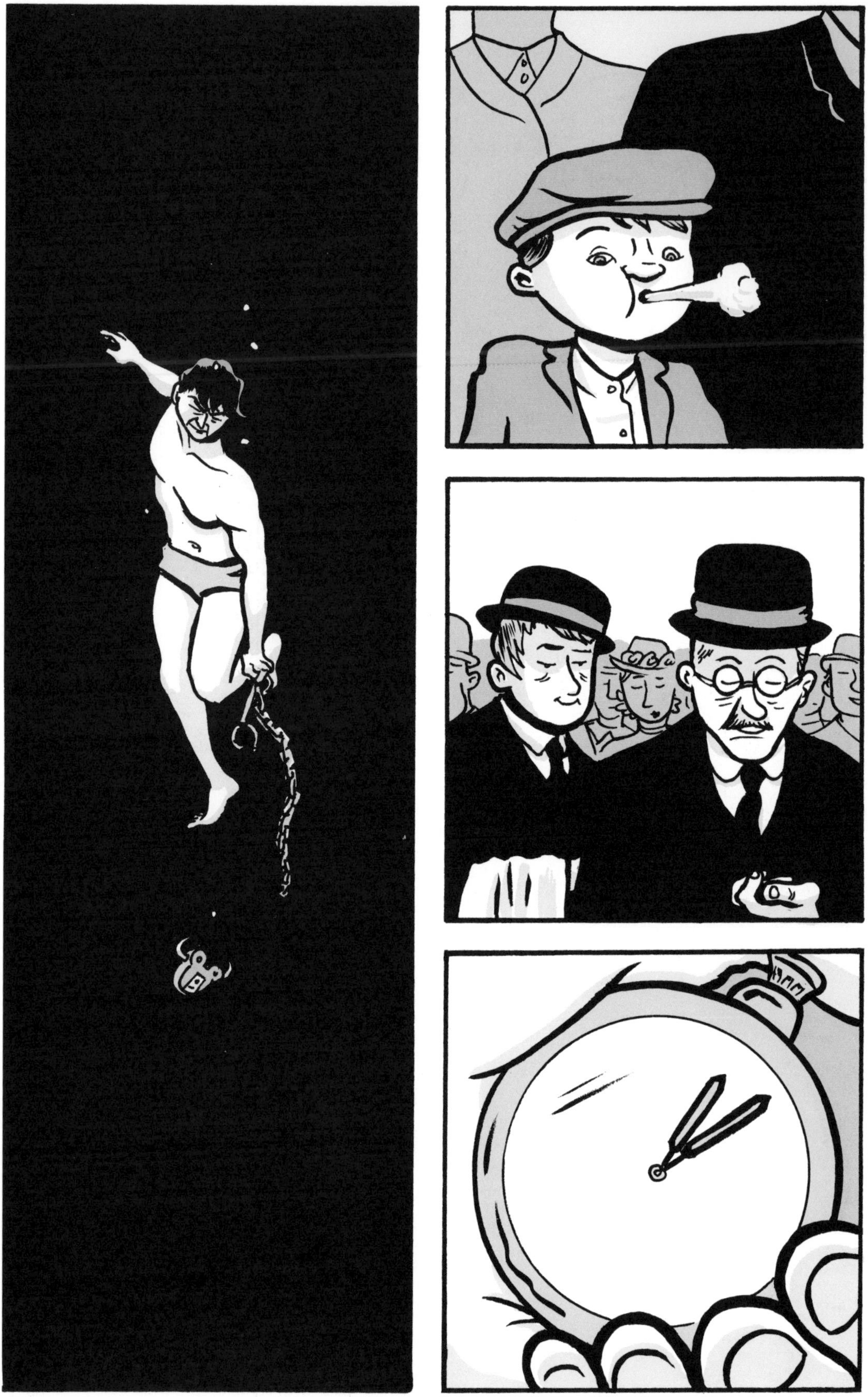

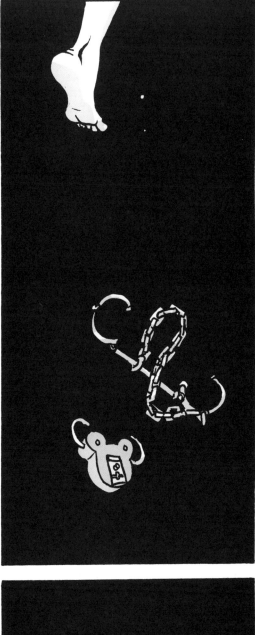

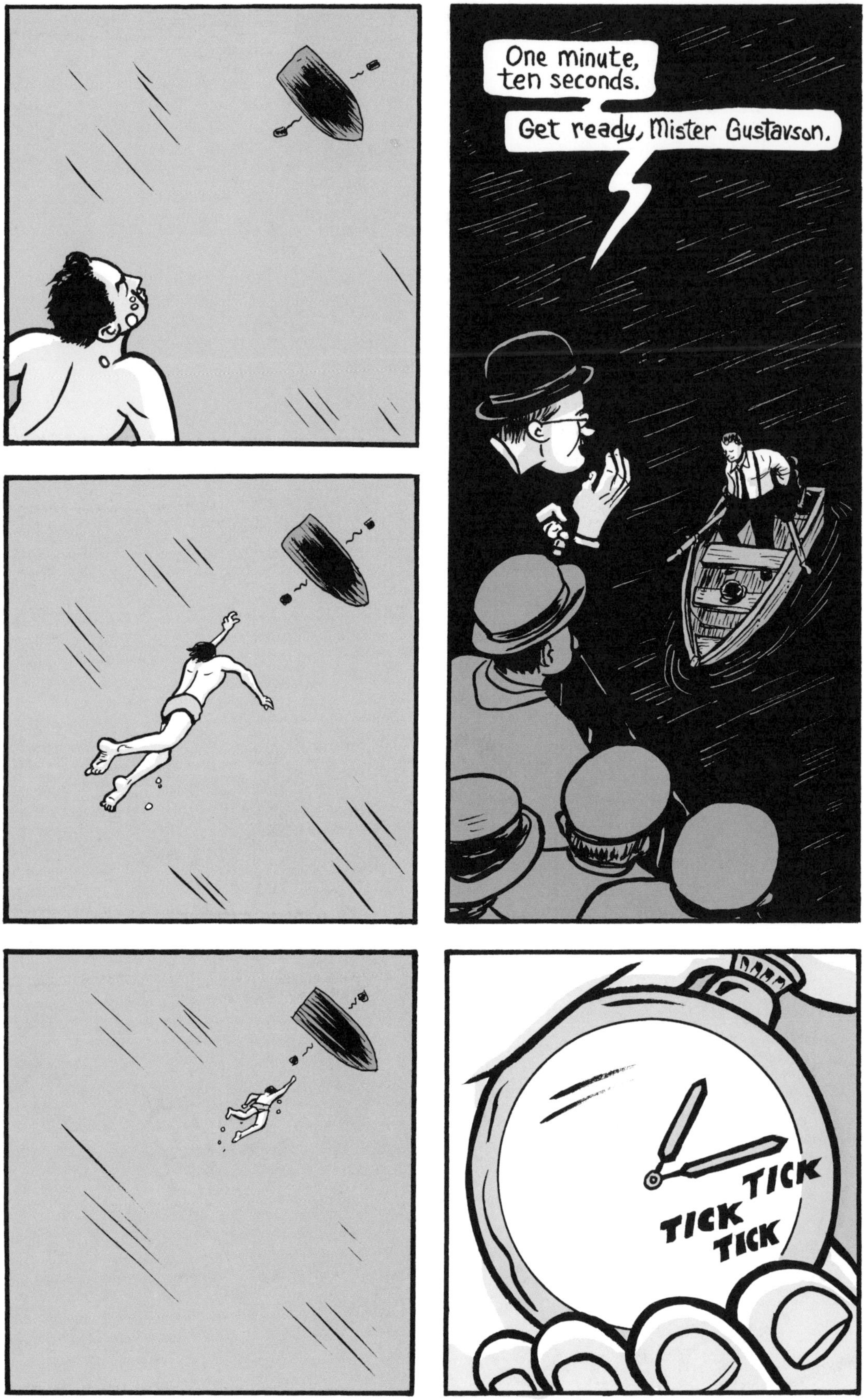
One minute, ten seconds.
Get ready, Mister Gustavson.
TICK
TICK
TICK

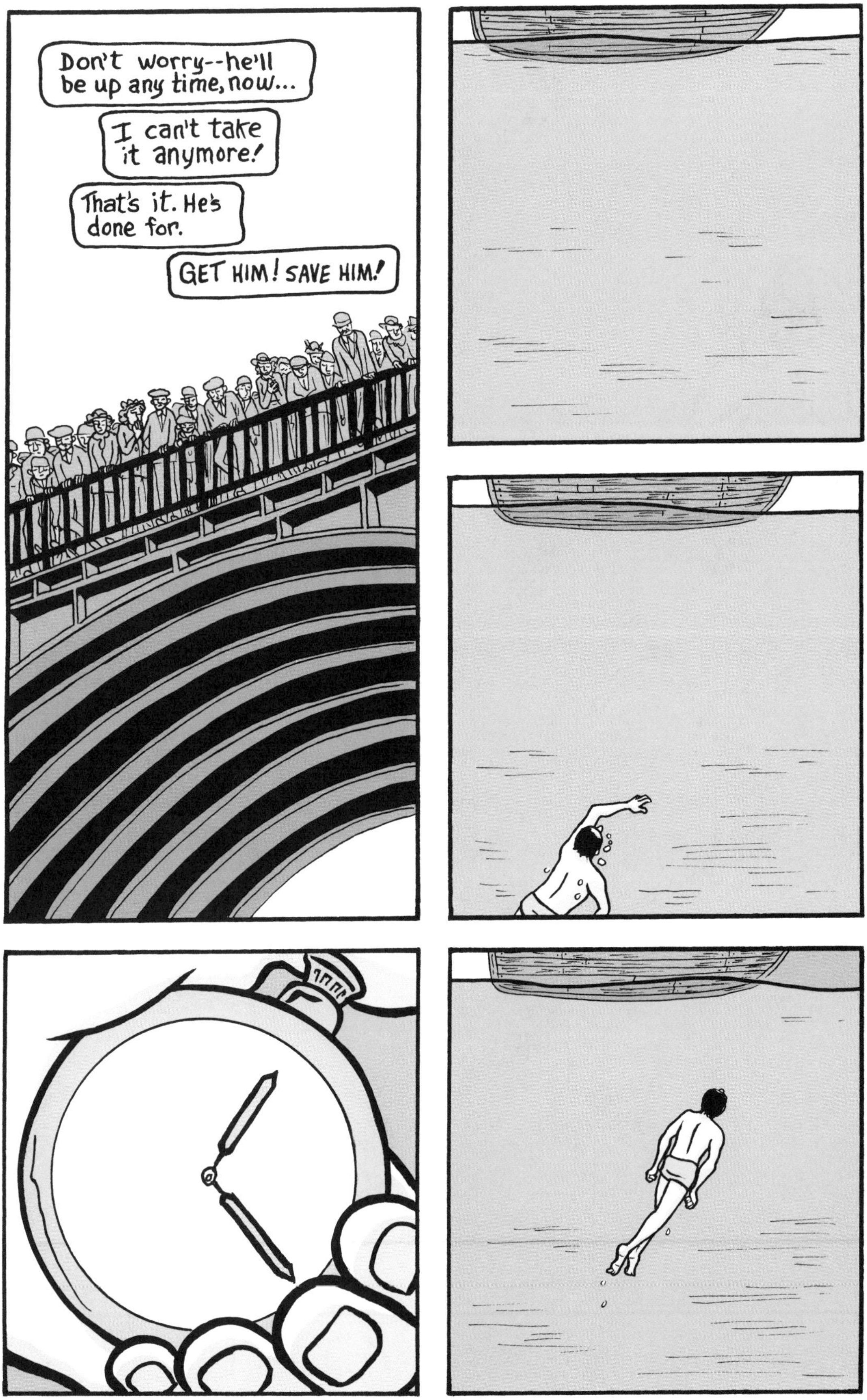
Don't worry--he'll be up any time, now...
I can't take it anymore!
That's it. He's done for.
GET HIM! SAVE HIM!

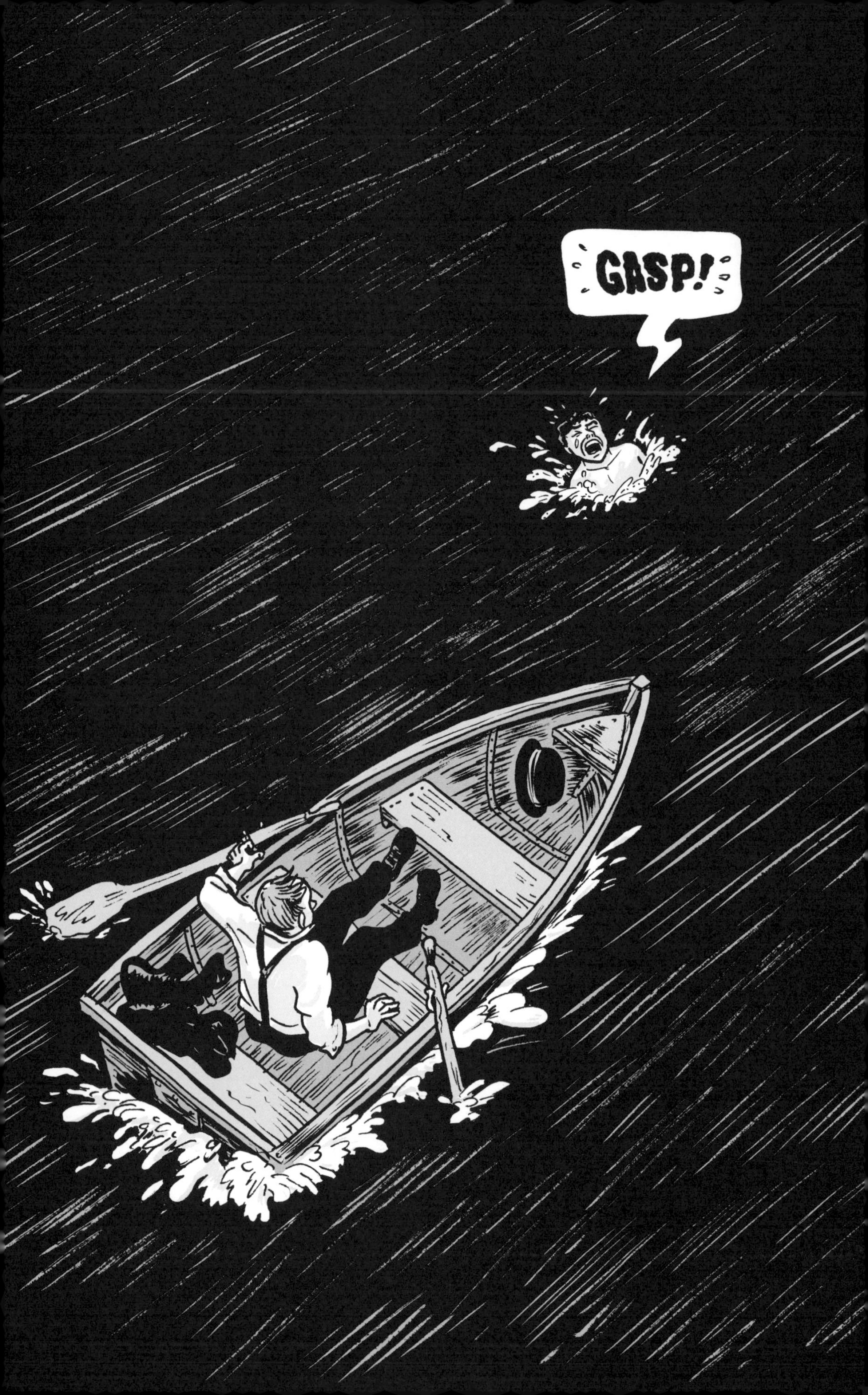
GASP!

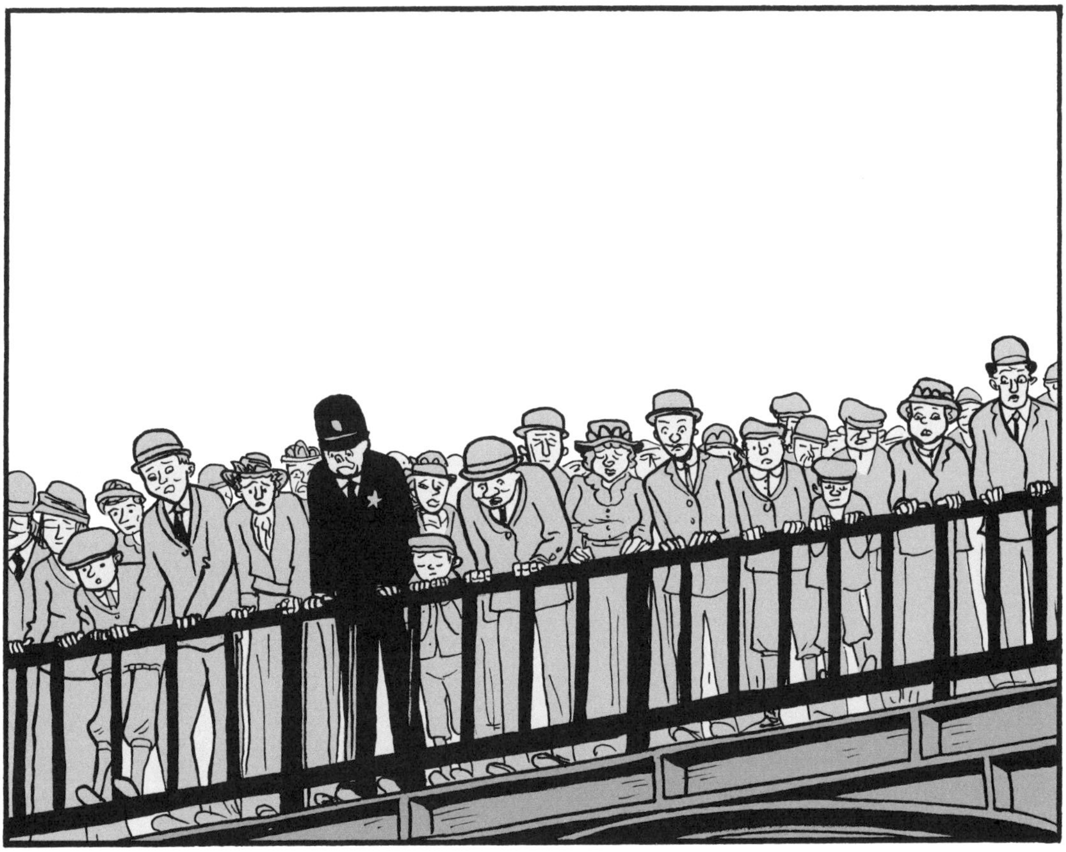

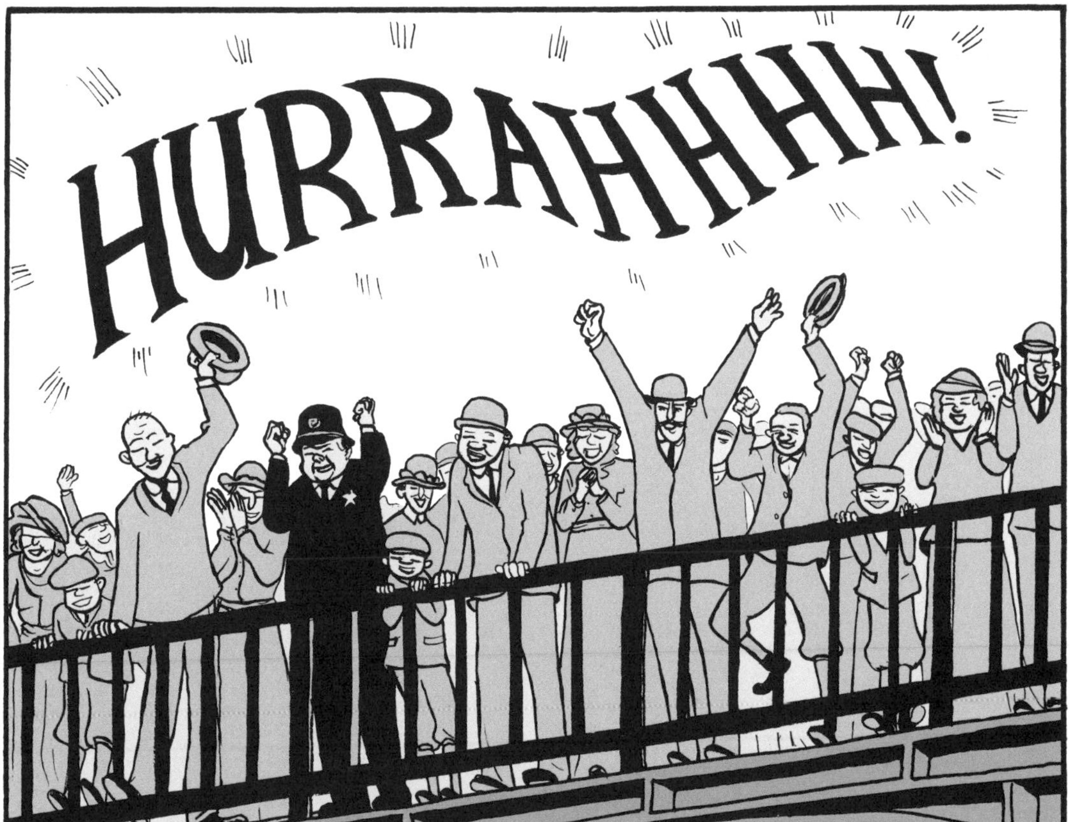
HURRAHHHH!

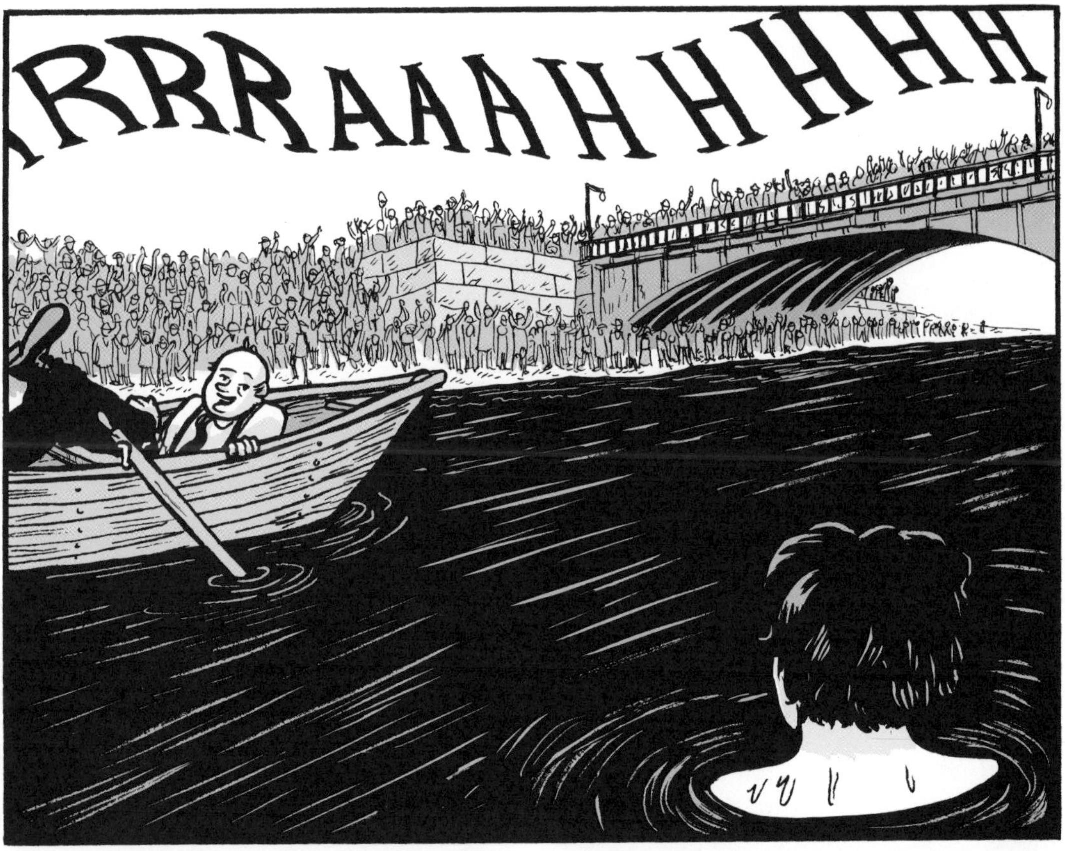
RRRAAAHHHHH

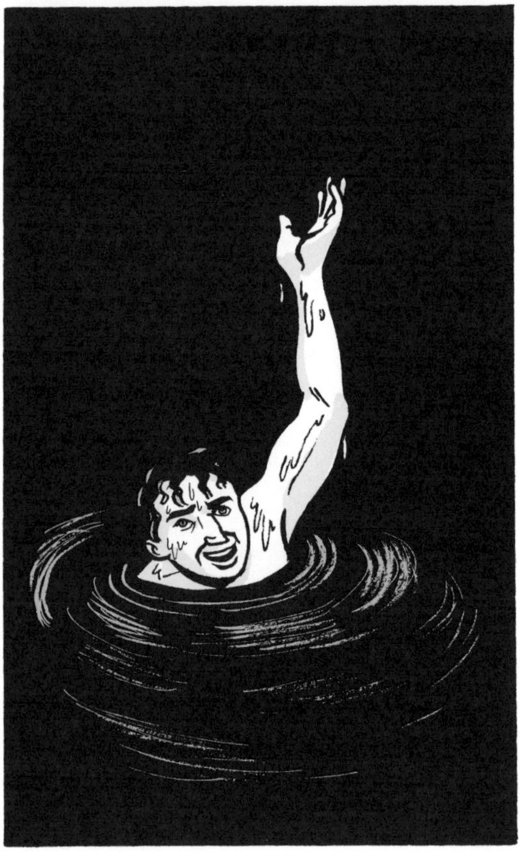

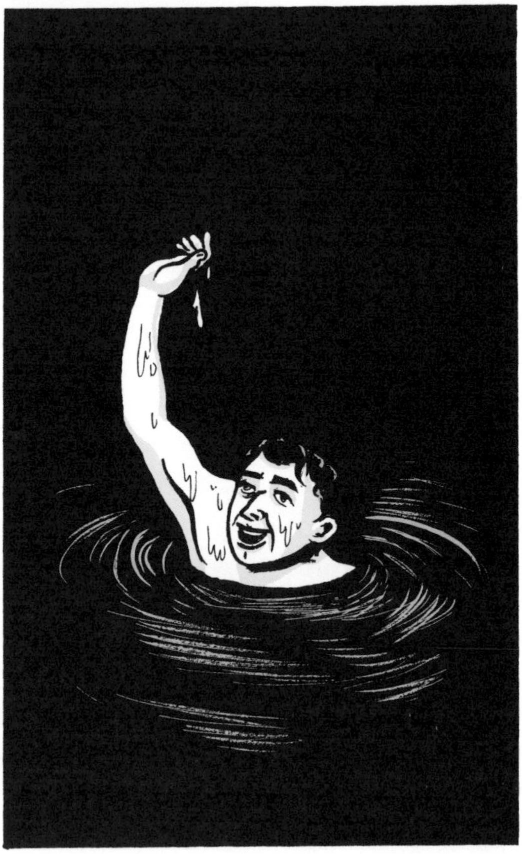

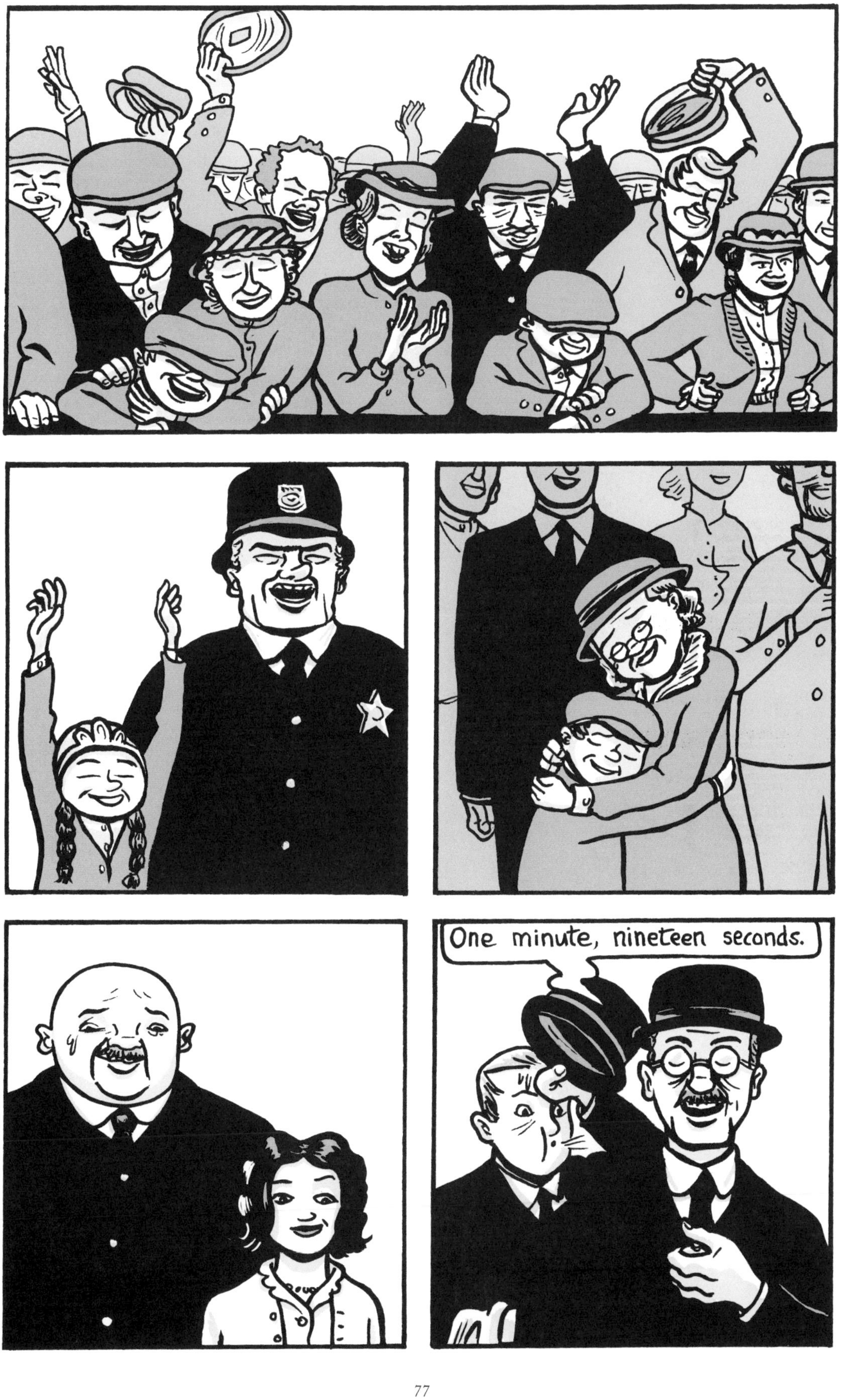
One minute, nineteen seconds.

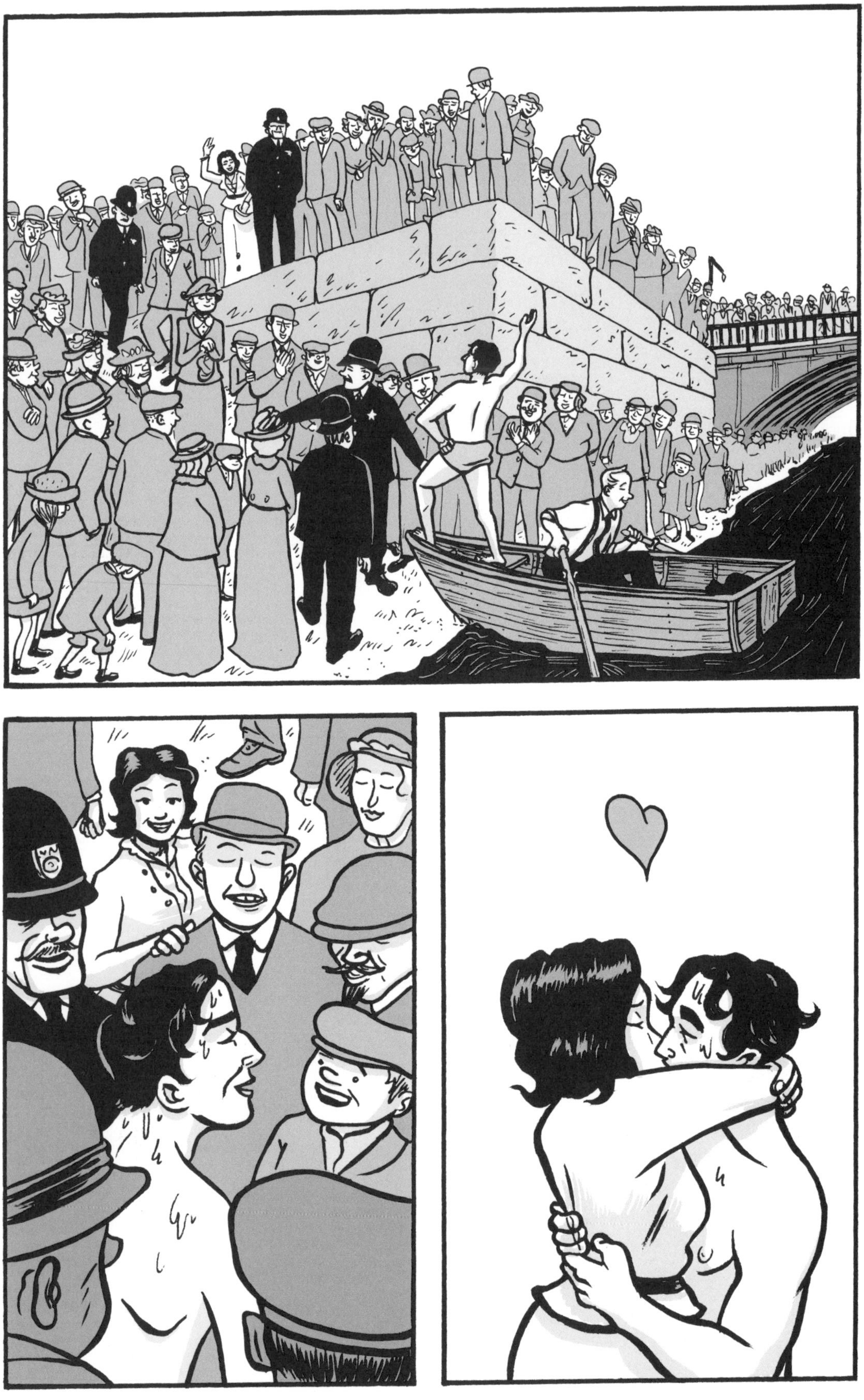

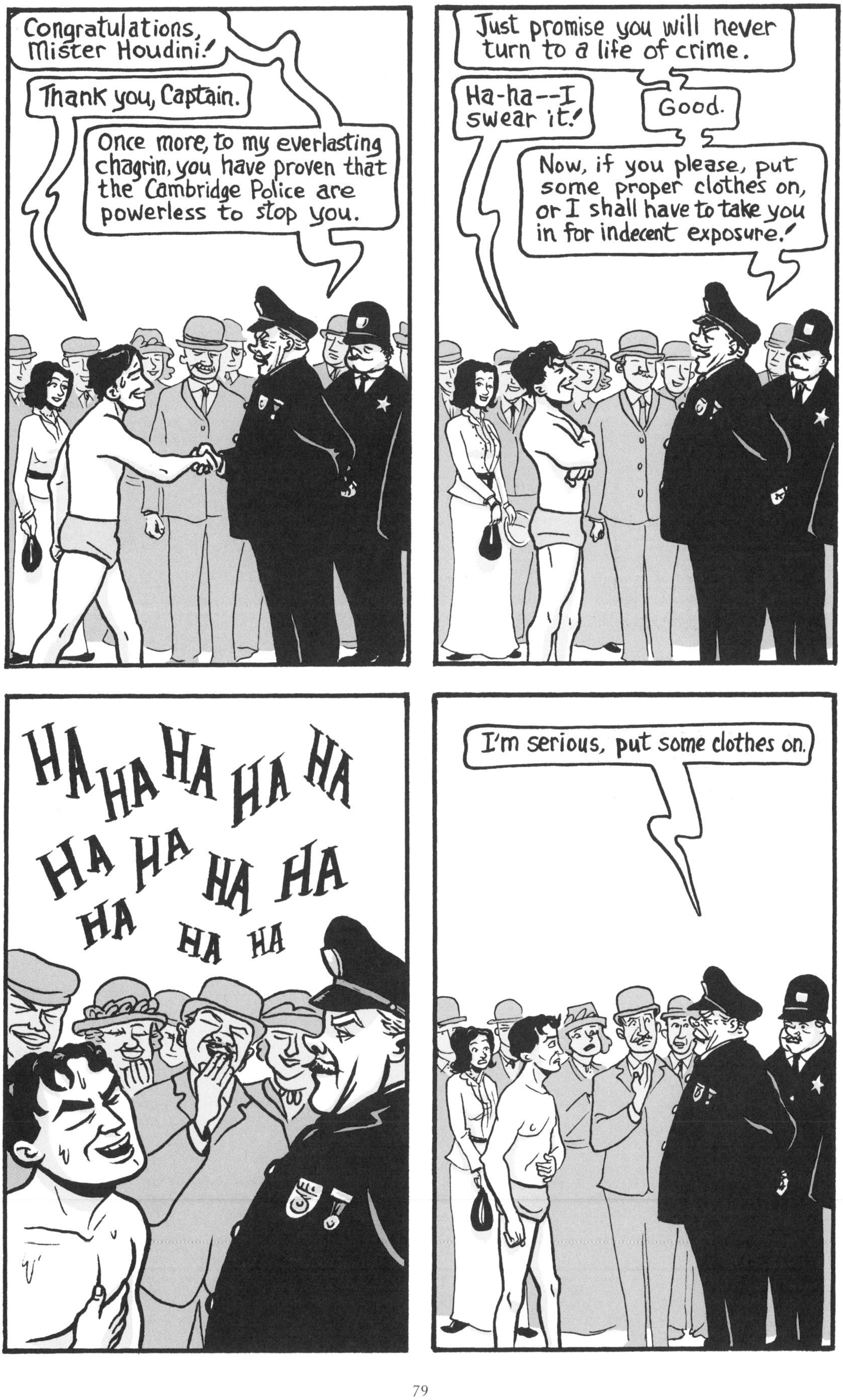
Congratulations, Mister Houdini!
Thank you, Captain.
Once more, to my everlasting chagrin, you have proven that the Cambridge Police are powerless to stop you.
Just promise you will never turn to a life of crime.
Ha-ha--I swear it!
Good.
Now, if you please, put some proper clothes on, or I shall have to take you in for indecent exposure!
HA HA HA HA HA HA
HA HA HA HA
HA HA HA
I'm serious, put some clothes on.

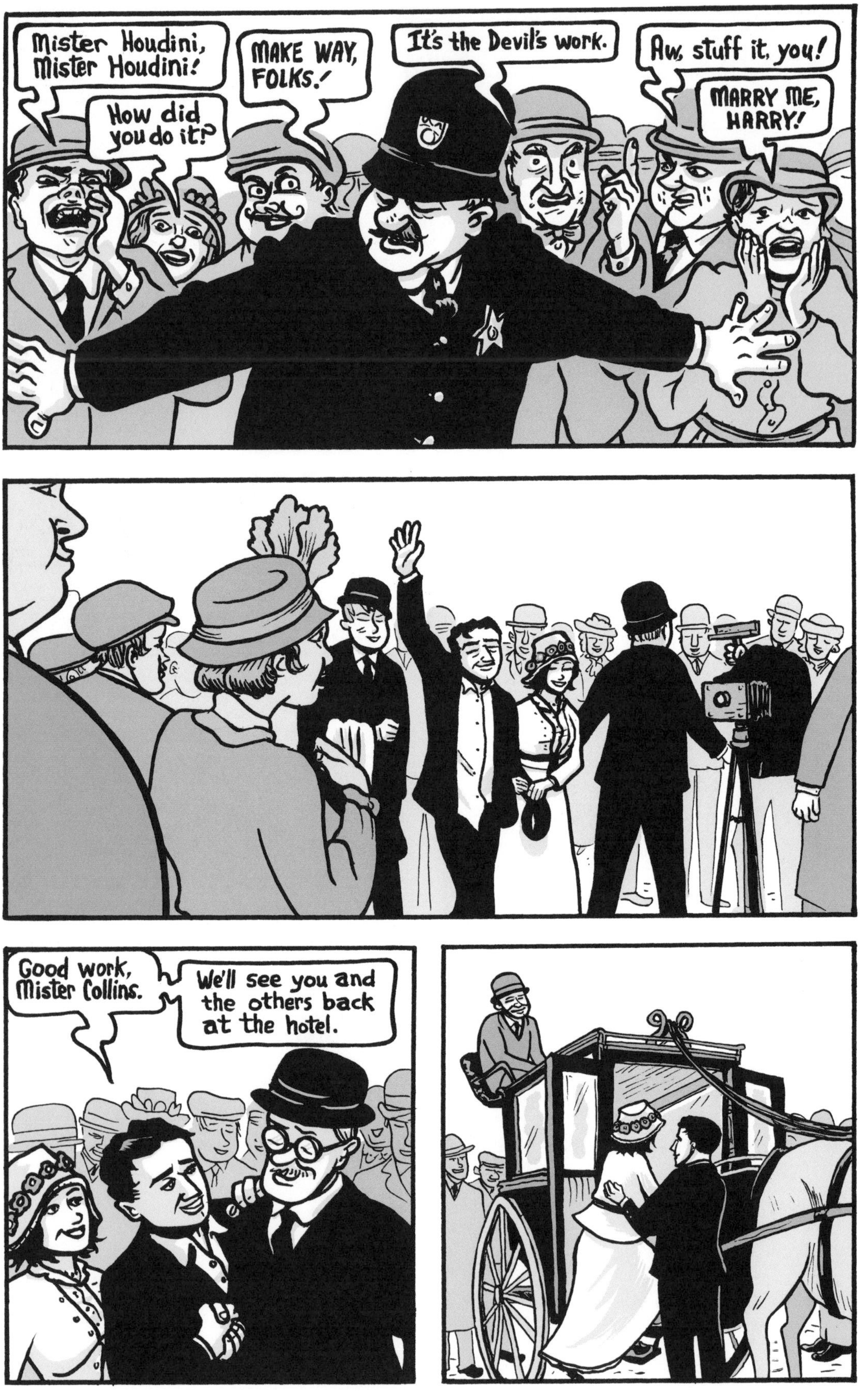
Mister Houdini, Mister Houdini!
How did you do it?
MAKE WAY, FOLKS.!
It's the Devil's work.
Aw, stuff it, you!
MARRY ME, HARRY!
Good work, Mister Collins.
We'll see you and the others back at the hotel.

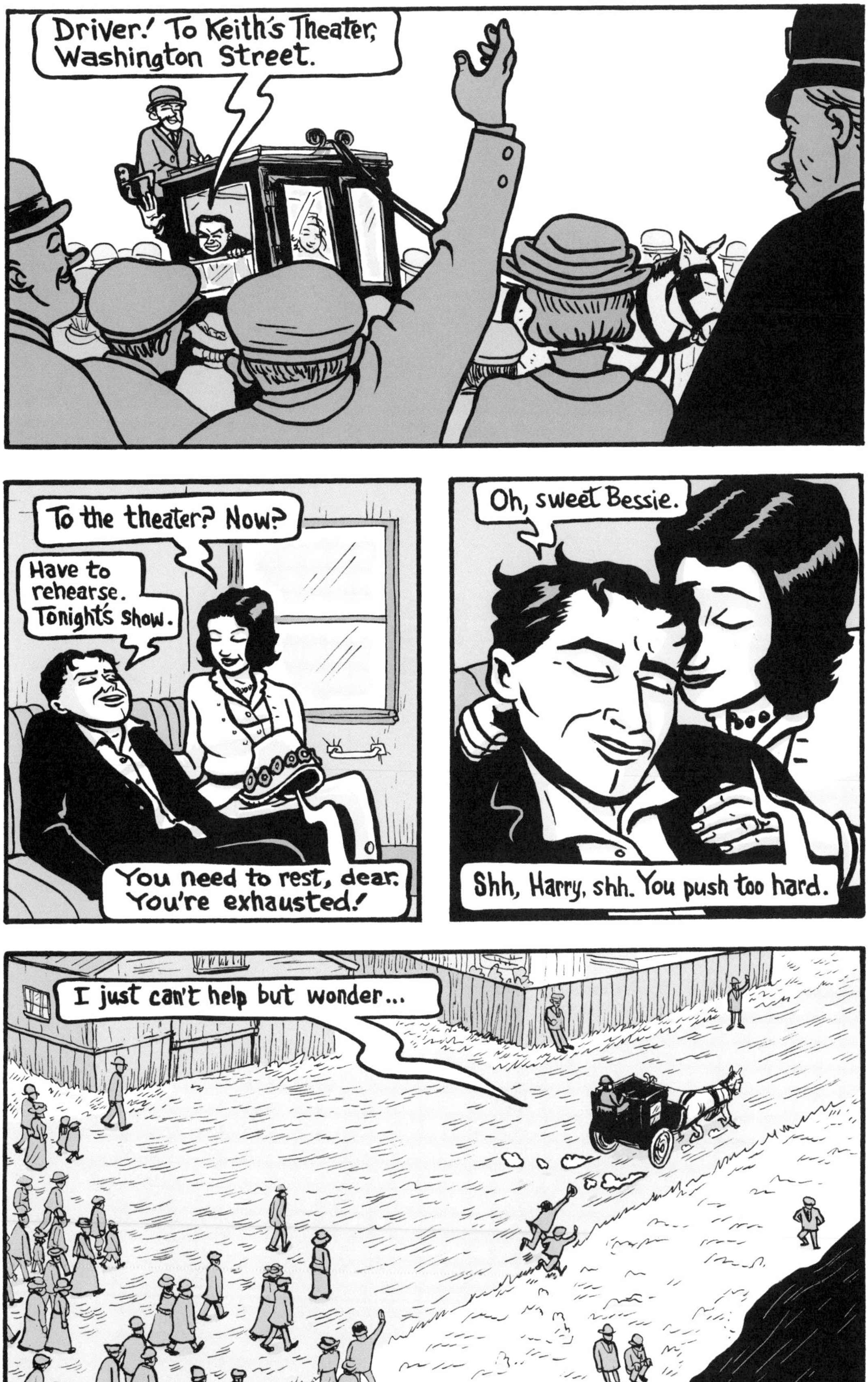
Driver! To Keith's Theater, Washington Street.
To the theater? Now?
Have to rehearse. Tonight's show.
You need to rest, dear. You're exhausted!
Oh, sweet Bessie.
Shh, Harry, shh. You push too hard.
I just can't help but wonder...

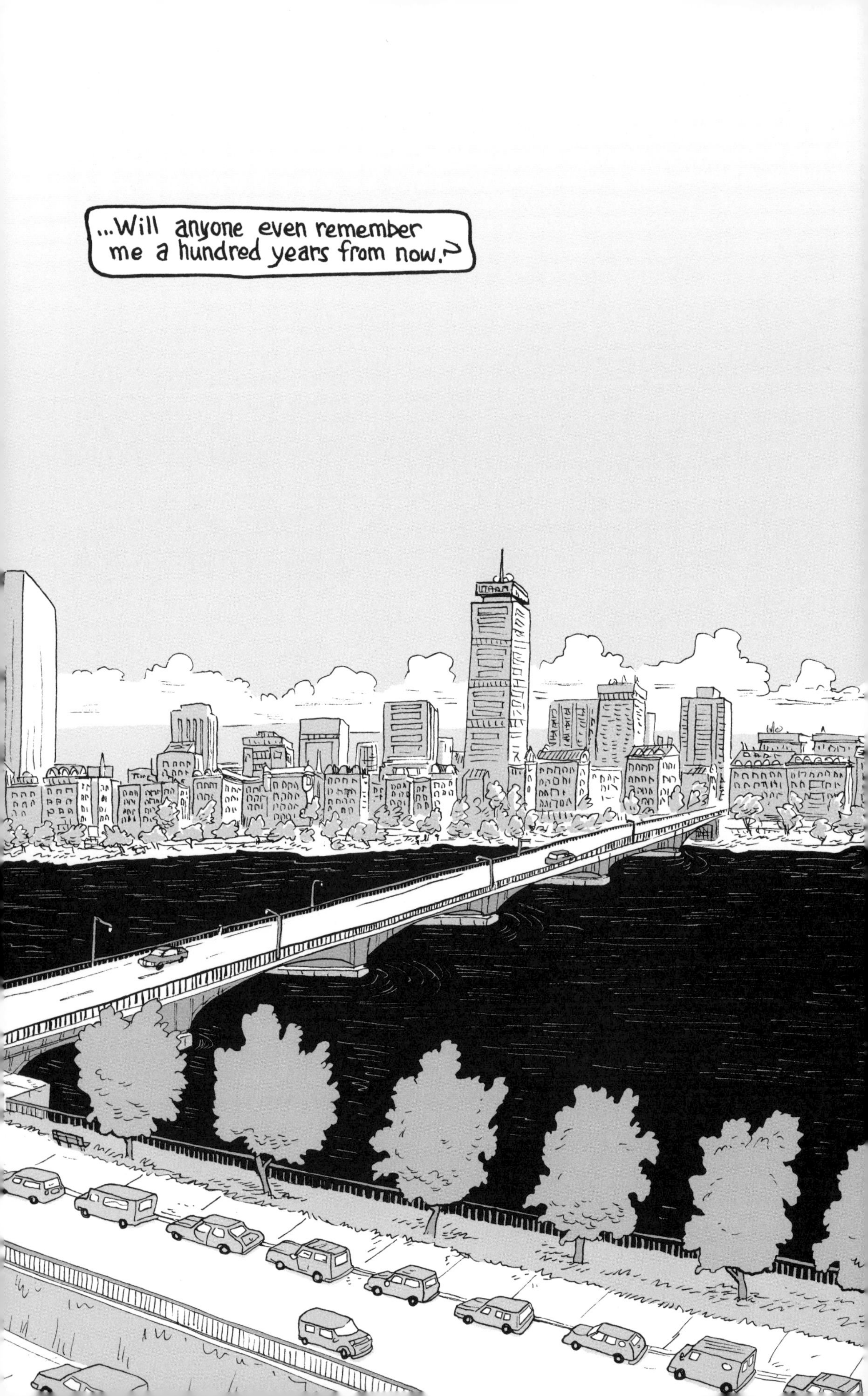
...Will anyone even remember me a hundred years from now?

Handcuff King
Panel Discussions

PAGE 2 : *Boston and Cambridge, Massachusetts, in 1908*

 Founded by Puritan settlers from England in the seventeenth century, by 1908 Boston was a major port and center of manufacturing. Throughout its history, Boston attracted workers from all over the world. Every third person was foreign-born, and three out of four were of non-English descent. Of those, the greatest number had come to the area from Canada, but there were also big communities of Irish, Italian, Russian, Polish, Norwegian, Danish, and Lithuanian immigrants. Boston was also home to a large African American population, many the descendants of people who had escaped slavery in the southern United States, or come north after the Emancipation Proclamation.

To house the hundreds of thousands of workers necessary to operate the city's textile mills and shoe factories, acres of open land were covered with wooden tenement houses. Rent for a three-room flat with no heat, lighting, running water, or indoor toilet cost around five dollars a month. The streets were filled with bicycles and horse-drawn carts and carriages that could reach top speed of a whopping eight to ten miles per hour. In 1853, the city established the first horse car transportation line (the precursor to the subway train) in the United States, which ran between Boston and Cambridge.

Boston's manufacturing went into a state of decline during the first decade of the twentieth century. The once-thriving factories and mills had become old and obsolete. Many such businesses closed and relocated to the South, replaced by service industries, banking and finance, and retailing and wholesaling.

PAGE 3 : *Locks of the Day and How Houdini Prepared to Pick Them*

 The word "handcuff" started out as "handcop." "To cop" means "to get a hold of," or "capture," which is why one slang term for "police officer" is "cop." Handcuffs were originally invented to limit the movements of prisoners and make it more difficult for them to escape. There is evidence that the Carthaginians used metal handcuffs around 2,400 years ago when they invaded Greece and took many captives alive. In Houdini's time, as in our own, policemen used metal handcuffs to restrain criminals or dangerous individuals. Today the police also use handcuffs made of extremely tough plastic.

From the earliest days of his career as a magician and escape artist, Houdini studied the inner workings of as many different locks as he could get his hands on. He took apart every new lock he encountered in order to study its internal mechanism and figure out the easiest way to pick it. To broaden his understanding, he would often seek the advice of professional locksmiths, and over time built an arsenal of tiny keys, lockpicks, and other tools to allow him to open the toughest locks with ease. If he had ever given up his career as a performer, he would have had no trouble at all getting work as a master locksmith! There is little doubt that if Houdini were alive today, he would be able to easily open any modern lock handed to him.

Since they are only intended as temporary restraints, handcuffs are generally not the hardest or most complicated of locks. Even though there were many different types of cuffs in use at the time by the various police forces of the world, Houdini could tell at a glance how a given pair operated, and what tool he would need to escape from them. Some cuffs could even be popped open if the captive struck them against a hard surface in the right place. On occasion, Houdini would conceal a steel plate underneath one pant leg for this purpose.

For any of his public escapes, Houdini or one of his assistants would find out in advance what sort of padlock, handcuff, or container would be used to hold him, and he would take every precaution to make sure he was properly equipped to make the escape. More often than not, he could escape within seconds of being confined, but he would drag out the process to maximize the dramatic effect of the performance. In the case of the Boston bridge jump shown in this story, Houdini probably knew well in advance what sort of cuffs the police would use, and even if he didn't, once he inspected them in public he would have instantly determined the best method by which to open them.

PAGE 7 : *Bess. Her History Onstage with Houdini, and How They Met*

As with many aspects of their lives together, the stories of how Bess Rahner and Harry Houdini met vary, but according to Bess it was in 1894, when she was eighteen and Houdini gave a show at her high school in Brooklyn, New York. Mrs. Rahner, Bess's mother—like many other people at that time—thought theatrical performances "wicked," and frowned on them. But Bess convinced her mother to let her attend, and sat with her in the front row on the day of the performance.

At one point in the act, the magician upset a bottle of acid being used as part of a trick, and some of it splashed off the stage and onto Bess's dress. Houdini was embarrassed and apologetic, but Mrs. Rahner was furious. Later, Houdini called on the Rahners to find out what size dress Bess wore, and his mother set about sewing a replacement. Bess was thrilled when Houdini brought the finished product back to her, and after putting it on, sneaked out to spend the day with him.

They planned to go to Coney Island, but

Bess became worried about how upset her mother would be when she learned of her going out without permission. Houdini said, "If you were my wife, they wouldn't dare punish you!" Bess was understandably surprised by this somewhat dramatic proposal of marriage, but before she knew what was happening, the two stepped into a secondhand jewelry store and bought a ring together. Caught up in the romance and strong feelings they felt for one another, they married that afternoon.

Bess became an integral part of Houdini's career from then on, acting as his assistant and co-performer in several of his most famous acts. She was an indispensable component of his fame and success throughout their days together. Their romantic and professional relationships were thoroughly entwined, and by all accounts their marriage was one of happiness and contentment.

Many people have speculated about the notion of Bess concealing a pick in her mouth to pass to Houdini by way of a kiss, but no one has ever proven it conclusively. It is impossible to know for sure, but we include it as a part of this story for dramatic purposes, because it might have happened that way, and it is symbolic of the immeasurable importance Bess Rahner had in the life and career of Harry Houdini.

PAGE 9 : *In the Early Part of the Twentieth Century Everybody Wore Hats*

From Colonial times up through the 1960s, American men and women commonly wore hats outdoors, all year round. In addition to shielding its wearer's head from the elements, a hat's style indicated a person's social status and even occupation. One of the most striking aspects of photographs of crowded streets in Houdini's time is that nearly everyone is wearing a hat. It's difficult to find a hatless individual among them. A hat was such an integral part of a person's wardrobe that going outside without one must have felt like going outside without your shoes on. A man would usually only take off his hat in public as a

sign of respect or humility.

Both men and women wore hats that conformed to the fashion trends of the time. Although women's hats had much more variety, men took pride in what they put on their heads as well, and milliners, or hatmakers, did very good business catering to the headgear needs of both men and women. Nowadays you can still find milliners practicing their trade, but not as many people wear hats as they did one hundred years ago.

PAGE 10 : *American Promotion and Advertising in 1908*

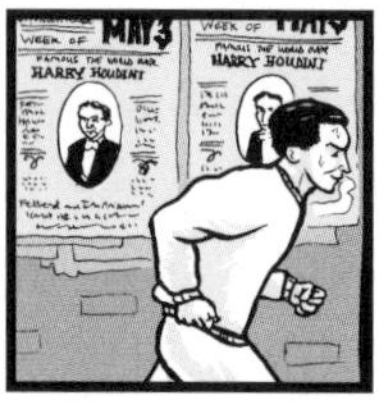

Before the Internet, television, and radio, the main way to promote a product, service, performance, or political candidate in America was through advertisement in printed media, such as newspapers, handbills, or posters. But a creative promoter would employ other means of seizing the public's attention, and Harry Houdini was nothing if not a creative promoter.

In addition to the forms of advertising shown in this story (all of which he actually used), Houdini used hired elephants, early motion pictures, and elaborate stunts to make his name known to as many people as possible. Performed for free in public, bridge jumps like the one depicted here were among the most effective ways Houdini could promote himself. The idea was that if enough people witnessed the event and were impressed, they would pay to see his theatrical show, or at least help spread his fame by telling their friends about the bridge jump.

PAGE 13 : *Anti-Semitism*

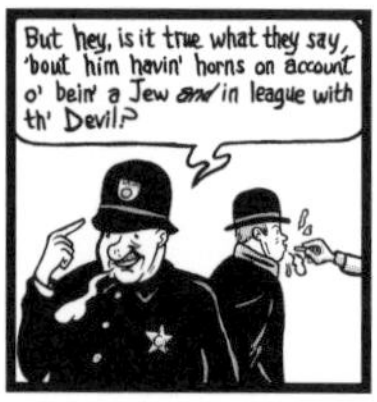
But hey, is it true what they say, 'bout him havin' horns on account o' bein' a Jew in league with th' Devil?

Houdini's real name was Ehrich Weiss. He always claimed to have been born in Appleton, Wisconsin, but the truth is that his family came to America from Budapest, Hungary, in 1874, when he was just a baby. The Weiss family was Jewish, and evidence suggests that they left Europe in part because of the discrimination they faced as Jews. They settled in Appleton because of a family connection to the sizable Jewish community there, and Ehrich's father became the rabbi of the town's first synagogue.

The myth that Jewish people have horns dates at least to the Middle Ages. People can often be afraid of things outside their understanding, and since a Christian worldview dominated Europe in those times, foreign ideas or people were often wrongly imagined to possess attributes of demons or the Devil. As has happened with many religious and ethnic minorities throughout history, negative stereotypes and false notions about Jewish people grew out of a fear of the unknown.

Houdini always considered himself an American first and only incidentally a Jew, and was lucky enough to encounter very little discrimination in his lifetime. During his first tour of Europe, he was appalled by the anti-Semitism he heard expressed by people who had no idea he was Jewish. This just reinforced his love for America, where freedom of religion and ideas is a founding principle, and almost everyone is originally from somewhere else.

PAGE 26 : *Reporters Couldn't E-mail or Fax Their Stories to the Newspapers*

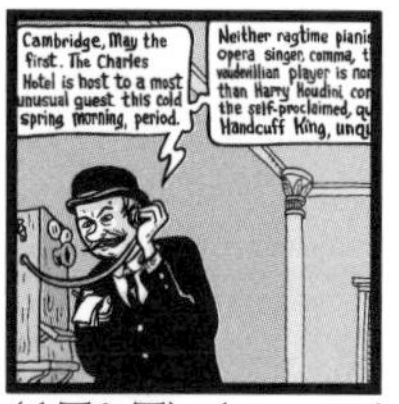
Cambridge, May the first. The Charles Hotel is host to a most unusual guest this cold spring morning, period.

Telephones were invented in 1876, and thirty-two years later, in 1908, not many people used them. The American Telephone and Telegraph Company (AT&T), America's largest phone company at the time, had been based in Boston until 1907, so there were more telephones in the Boston metropolitan area than any other city besides New York.

Telephones required connection to a special telephone cable (similar to today's landlines), and in 1908 the network of this cable didn't even reach all the way across the country. Someone making a call from Boston wouldn't be able to reach anyone farther west than Omaha, Nebraska, and even then, he or she would only be able to call a big city, since many small towns didn't even have a single telephone yet. Most homes didn't have a telephone until the 1920s or 1930s.

It's safe to assume that a good hotel in the Boston area would have had at least one telephone for guests to use. Mr. Smith, the reporter who calls in his story from the hotel telephone, could have sent his message by telegraph, but he would have had to have found a telegraph office to send the message via Morse code. Even though voice transmission was slow and of poor quality (often with an echo effect), a telephone was still the quickest and most direct way to communicate over a long distance.

PAGE 33 : *Houdini's Need for Utter Secrecy and the Measures He Took to Ensure It*

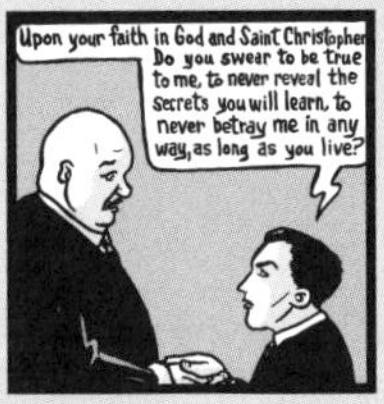
Upon your faith in God and Saint Christopher
Do you swear to be true to me, to never reveal the secrets you will learn, to never betray me in any way, as long as you live?

The less Houdini's audience knew about how he accomplished a given feat, the more amazing it seemed to them. So Houdini's success depended on the fact that he and his assistants (and Bess) knew things that his audience did not know. To ensure that the public was continually astounded by the seemingly impossible things he accomplished, he took great pains to keep his methods hidden. The scene in this story where Houdini makes Mister Beatty swear his loyalty is indicative of how seriously Houdini treated this issue. Only the most trustworthy individuals were allowed into his inner circle, and all were sworn to complete secrecy in a similar manner.

Perhaps the most striking aspect of Houdini's career is that all of his accomplishments were the result of sheer physical and mental dedication. When people asked him if magic or the supernatural were involved in his act, he always strongly denied it, asserting that his success was simply the result of diligent study, extraordinary self-discipline, and intense physical training. He was essentially saying, "Anyone could do what I do if they worked hard enough." Of course, no one in Houdini's time or since has worked as hard as he did to the same end.

Over the years, the secrets of many of Houdini's tricks have become public knowledge, but even to this day some of his feats cannot be conclusively explained by experts in stage magic or escapology.

PAGE 52 : *There Were No Sound Systems or Microphones*

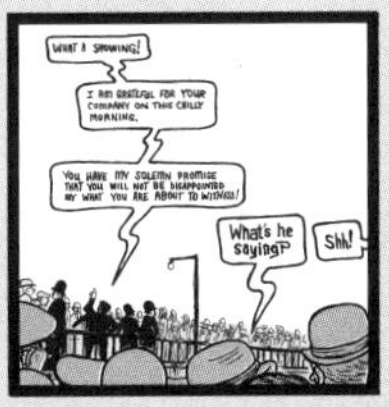
What's he saying?
Shh!

In 1908, the only real way to amplify your voice in public was to use a megaphone, which at the time was just a stiff paper cone that you would hold up to your mouth and shout through. There were no electric sound systems or other technological means by which to increase the volume of a person's speaking voice. Houdini liked to maintain a personal connection with his audience, and since a megaphone is large enough to obscure the speaker's face when in use, and there are no photographs showing Houdini using one, it is likely that he always spoke without amplification.

Public speakers, with or without megaphones, had to be "loud and clear" in their delivery in order to communicate to the largest possible number of people over the greatest possible distance. Huge crowds of people listening to a good public speaker would remain almost utterly silent in order to hear what was being said, but would often shout back whenever there was an appropriate pause in the speech, or when they agreed or disagreed with something the speaker said.

PAGE 53 : *An Early College Rivalry*

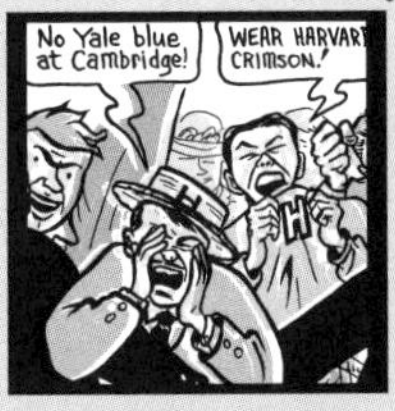
No Yale blue at Cambridge!
WEAR HARVAR CRIMSON!

The town of Cambridge, just across the Charles River from Boston proper, was home to MIT (the Massachusetts Institute of Technology) and Harvard University, making it one of the foremost centers of higher learning in the United States. Harvard's traditional rival was Yale University, in nearby New Haven, Connecticut, which is why the students in the story demand that Houdini change the color of his bathing trunks. Houdini, always the showman, knew how to exploit the rivalry of the schools to his best advantage.

PAGES 60-78 : ***The Magician's Professional Code***

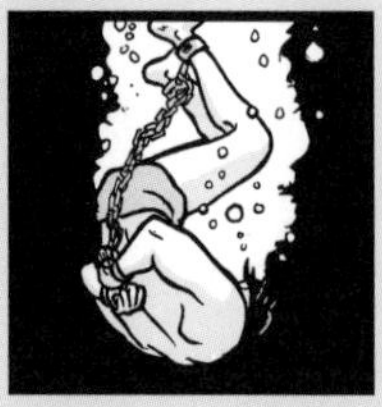

Because none of the actual cartoonists who helped make this book are professional magicians, we can reveal (or at least suggest) one of Houdini's secrets. Professional magicians are never ever supposed to reveal how a trick or an illusion is pulled off.

PAGE 82 : ***Fame***

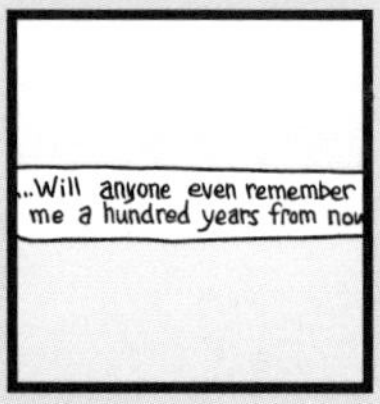
..Will anyone even remember me a hundred years from no

Houdini's preoccupation with fame did not go to waste. Houdini has been featured in hundreds of books, movies, plays, and television programs. So many people seem to be famous for a short amount of time. Houdini died in 1926 and is still famous today.

Bibliography

Berlin, Irving, and Mike Nicholson. "Marie from Sunny Italy," 1907.

Brandon, Ruth. *The Life and Many Deaths of Harry Houdini*. Random House, New York, 1993.

Christopher, Milbourne. *Houdini: The Untold Story*. Thomas Y. Crowell Company, New York, 1969.

Eras, Vincent J. M. *Locks and Keys Throughout the Ages*. H. H. Fronczek, Amsterdam, 1957.

Gresham, William Lindsay. *Houdini: The Man Who Walked Through Walls*. Henry Holt and Co., New York, 1959.

Harlow, Alvin F. *Old Wires and New Waves (History of the Telegraph, Telephone, and Wireless)*. Appleton-Century, New York, 1936.

Silverman, Kenneth, *Houdini!!!: The Career of Ehrich Weiss*, Perennial (HarperCollins), New York, 1997.

Credits

WRITER

Jason Lutes is a cartoonist living in Vermont. He has been an admirer of Houdini for most of his adult life. Once, he taught himself a bunch of card tricks, but please don't ask him to perform any of them, because he'll just embarrass himself.

ARTIST

Nick Bertozzi has managed to trick the world into believing he is an award-winning cartoonist. He escaped from an isolation tank and into the arms of a beautiful family that lives a mile from Houdini's grave in Queens, New York. He is hard at work on new feats as you read this.

INTRODUCTION

Glen David Gold is the author of the memoir *I Will Be Complete* and the novels *Sunnyside* and *Carter Beats the Devil*, an international best seller currently available in fourteen languages. He has written about comic books and magic for exhibition catalogues and journals such as the *New York Times Magazine*.

SERIES EDITOR

James Sturm has been sawed in half, pulled from a top hat, and is a cartoonist and the cofounder of the Center for Cartoon Studies. His graphic novels include *Satchel Paige: Striking Out Jim Crow*, *The Golem's Mighty Swing*, *Market Day*, and *Off Season*. His picture books for children include *Ape and Armadillo Take Over the World*, *Birdsong*, and the Adventures in Cartooning series (with Andrew Arnold and Alexis Frederick-Frost).

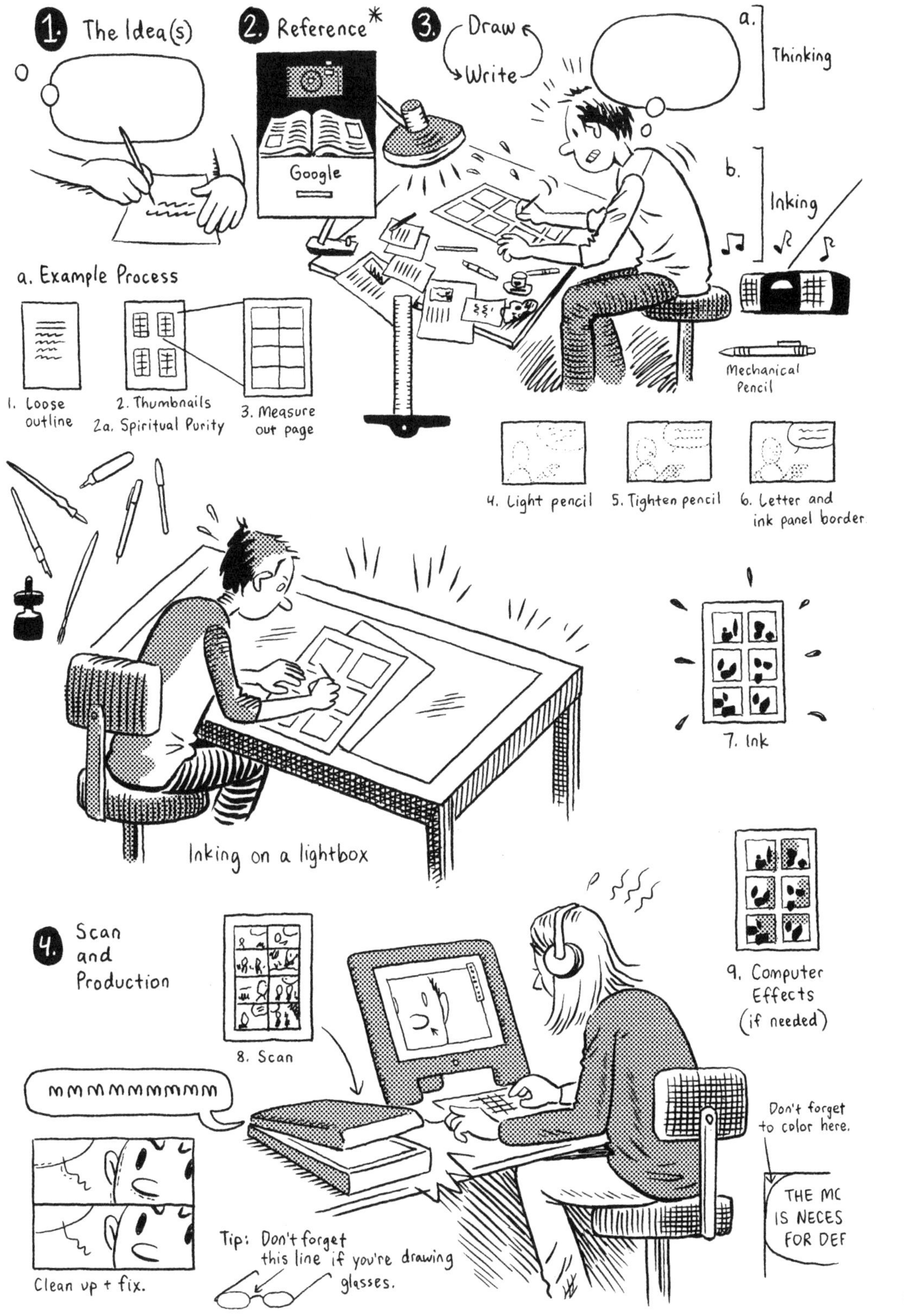
1. The Idea(s)
2. Reference*
Google
3. Draw
Write
a. Thinking
b. Inking
a. Example Process
1. Loose outline
2. Thumbnails
2a. Spiritual Purity
3. Measure out page
Mechanical Pencil
4. Light pencil
5. Tighten pencil
6. Letter and ink panel border
7. Ink
Inking on a lightbox
4. Scan and Production
8. Scan
9. Computer Effects (if needed)
mmmmmmmmmm
Don't forget to color here.
THE MC
IS NECES
FOR DEF
Clean up + fix.
Tip: Don't forget this line if you're drawing glasses.

Illustration this page: Kevin Huizenga

the CENTER for CARTOON STUDIES
CCS
White River Junction, Vermont
VISIT WWW.CARTOONSTUDIES.ORG

THE CENTER FOR CARTOON STUDIES produces comics, zines, posters, and graphic novels (like this book about Houdini!). For those interested in making comics themselves one day, the Center for Cartoon Studies is also America's finest cartooning school—offering one- and two-year courses of study, master of fine arts degrees, and summer workshops.